WHAT IS
WRONG
WITH PEOPLE?!

WHAT IS
WRONG
WITH PEOPLE?!

MARK LUTZ

Mill City Press, Minneapolis

Acknowledgments

Thanks to the Snell sisters. First of all, my wife, Elizabeth, for guarding my integrity by ensuring that I practice at home what I teach others to do. Your constant decision to be my number one fan was especially helpful in accomplishing this project. To Ginny, for your enthusiasm and affirmations and for your multiple proof readings and editorial suggestions. Your thoughts made this book much more readable. And to Gail for your technology expertise and enthusiasm when I was just about worn out by it all.

Thanks to the many members of the Vineyard Cincinnati Growth & Healing ministry. It was in the context of our community and our co-laboring that these ideas were shaped and refined. Special thanks to Sue Stiles, Gerry Spears and Joyce Carroll. I could not have had a better staff to work with. You helped keep me just this side of sanity while we dealt with the craziness in the world.

Thanks to my friend Jesus for your patience working with me and your determination to see all of us be who we are meant to be.

Contents

Introduction   1

1. Getting to the Source   3

2. Second Impact   13

3. Assessing The Damage   35

4. For Injury, There is Healing   49

5. For Immaturity, There is Nurturing   75

6. For Habits, There are Disciplines   81

7. For Oppression, There is Deliverance   87

8. Toto, We're Not in Kansas Anymore!   99

9. Escape from Crazyville   109

10. Last Thoughts   117

Introduction

I frequently find the behavior of people to be irritating. Even that guy looking back at me in the mirror each morning aggravates me regularly. I'm guessing this is true for many of us. Though we may have this frustration in common, we may have different points of interest when it comes to humanity's increasingly questionable and destructive attitudes and behaviors. For some, the burning question is, "I have this annoying co-worker/relative/ neighbor. How do I deal with the frustration caused by the people around me?" Others may be wrestling with the concern, "What's wrong with me that I keep recreating the same messes over and over again?" And fortunately there are those people who are in the place to be able to ask, "What can be done to help someone caught in patterns that are hurtful to self and others?"

Personally, I think all three are valid questions deserving of an answer. One is not necessarily more noble than the other. The perspective we have is influenced by the experiences we've had, negative or positive and the support that has or has not been available to us. When any of these is the authentic expression of what someone is experiencing, I love to try to help that person find a satisfying answer. That is in fact the intention of this book, to address the frustrations felt as a result of other people's actions as well as our own and to offer some ideas about what remedy might be possible.

In writing this book, I reviewed and considered my experiences with people over the course of my life's work. For about twenty years now, I have been the director and pastor over the recovery ministry for our church. What began as a few support/recovery groups has grown to around twenty-five to thirty such groups offered three times annually, touching almost a thousand people in a year's time.

We have trained hundreds of people to safely and effectively facilitate groups. My staff, coaches and I have spent countless hours supervising the volunteer group leaders in our ministry. Over and over again, we see that our attempts to help others must be preceded by our willingness to address our own condition first. From our collective experiences growing and healing and assisting others to do the same, we began to piece together an understanding around the question, *"What goes wrong in the human spirit that allows us to do crazy, hurtful things?"* What we have learned through these years, is shared here. I hope this will offer a useful framework and strategy, whichever perspective is of pressing interest to you now. I pray that in these pages you find hope and a plan for the part of the journey that is most relevant for you.

1

Getting to the Source

Do you ever find yourself asking, "What is *wrong* with people?!" I do! Driving down the freeway, a car darts across three lanes of traffic, narrowly missing the front end of my truck. I see the driver talking on a cell phone, and wonder, "What is *wrong* with people?" When I see a news program about children being neglected or abused, I wonder, "What is *wrong* with people?!" When the evening news tells of a high-speed car chase that ends with the driver, his children in car seats, arrested for possession of drugs, I am dumbfounded and incensed. "What is *wrong* with people?!" I shout at my television.

Growing up, I was told to behave and to not be a bad boy. I was told that a lot; by parents, Sunday school teachers and other adults in authority. My interpretation was, "If I *do* bad things then I *am* a bad person." As the years went by, I continued to live out of this conclusion that because I continue to make occasional bad decisions and act badly, I must be bad at my core. With each internal assertion that this must be true, with each repetition, the belief grew stronger. It grew strong enough that it could operate at a subconscious level. I didn't even need to have the words form an internal dialogue. I would just feel "less than" whenever I would act apart from the values that had been instilled in me. Now, those thoughts that I internalized about myself long ago are projected onto others in my moments of moral outrage. I make the judgment when I see or hear about these reports of deplorable behavior that this must be another case of a bad person, doing bad things.

I think this belief that if I do bad, I am bad is prevalent among us. But is it really true? There are certainly still plenty of times when I have lapses of patience, consideration or kindness. I have my moments of selfishness. Does this mean I am bad? Is this what is wrong with me and why I do the things I do? It certainly feels much more empowering to ask, "What is wrong with *those* people?" from a place of moral superiority, than it is to question, "What is wrong with *me*?" from the depths of my shame spiral. I wonder, is either use of the question really all that productive?

Perhaps, there is a profitable purpose in asking the question, "What *is* wrong with people (including me)?" What if I asked the question in another tone, for a reason other than venting a cathartic rant that serves as the prelude to my moral judgment? What if I asked the question out of curiosity and in the hope of gaining understanding? What if greater understanding led me to deeper wholeness myself? What if I, being more sound of mind, soul and spirit could become a change agent in the culture around me? Might it then be worthwhile to ask, "What is *wrong* with people?"

As we try to understand the human condition, we need to see beyond the conventional thinking that people *do* bad things because they *are* bad. Certainly, volition plays a part in the outrageous behaviors we see. But what if there is more at work? What if there are factors that impinge upon a person's free will? This would certainly be important to account for, wouldn't it? Is there anything that could possibly influence our free will so strongly as to explain the horrific behaviors we see in the world around us?

The Bible tells an interesting story that may yield some valuable clues. It seems we have all been born into a world at war. There was already a battle between good and evil well underway by the time we showed up. In the book of Revelation Chapter 12 we read:

> *⁷And there was war in heaven. Michael and his angels fought against the dragon, and the dragon and his angels fought back. ⁸But he was not strong enough, and they lost their place in heaven. ⁹The great dragon was hurled down—that ancient serpent called the devil, or Satan, who leads the whole world astray. He was hurled to the earth, and his angels with him.*
>
> *¹⁰Then I heard a loud voice in heaven say: "Now have come the salvation and the power and the kingdom of our God, and the authority of his Christ.*

*For the accuser of our brothers, who accuses them
before our God day and night, has been hurled down.
[11]They overcame him by the blood of the Lamb and
by the word of their testimony; they did not love their
lives so much as to shrink from death.*

*[12]Therefore rejoice, you heavens and you who
dwell in them! But woe to the earth and the sea,
because the devil has gone down to you! He is filled
with fury, because he knows that his time is short."*

*[13]When the dragon saw that he had been hurled
to the earth, he pursued the woman who had given
birth to the male child. [14]The woman was given the
two wings of a great eagle, so that she might fly to the
place prepared for her in the desert, where she would
be taken care of for a time, times and half a time,
out of the serpent's reach. [15]Then from his mouth
the serpent spewed water like a river, to overtake the
woman and sweep her away with the torrent. [16]But
the earth helped the woman by opening its mouth
and swallowing the river that the dragon had spewed
out of his mouth. [17]Then the dragon was enraged
at the woman and went off to make war against
the rest of her offspring—those who obey God's
commandments and hold to the testimony of Jesus.*

WOW! What a story! The only things missing are a
couple of explosions and a car chase! This is like some great
cosmic bar brawl that spills out into the streets and turns
into a riot, except that it started in Heaven and spilled

onto the earth. Did you catch the part about "rejoicing in Heaven—but woe to those on the earth"? It is comforting to know the Angels are going, "Yea! The devil got thrown out of Heaven, down to earth!" Good for the angels! Not so good for us!

We find out Satan was thrown down to earth, and he is *"filled with fury."* He is not just mad, he is furious; he is livid; he is out-of-control insane with anger, and he is looking for someone to take it out on. He is enraged and making war against the offspring of the woman. He is waging war against those who obey God's commandments and hold to the testimony of Jesus. This sure goes a long way toward explaining why bad things happen to good people, doesn't it?

In this great cosmic war, Satan inflicts evil upon mankind. Satan incites evil amongst mankind. Satan corrupts creation so that evil becomes the natural consequence of destructive actions set in motion long ago.

Satan inflicts evil upon mankind. The New Testament is filled with stories of people that Jesus rescued from dark, spiritual influence. In the Gospel of Mark, Chapter 5, is the story of a man who suffered from an unclean or evil spirit. He lived among the tombs. He ran around naked, crying out and cutting himself with stones. People attempted to contain him by putting him in chains but he repeatedly broke out of his shackles. After one encounter with Jesus, the people found the man sitting, clothed and in his right mind next to Jesus. In the same Gospel, in Chapter 9, a man brings his son to Jesus. The son is reported to also

7

be afflicted with an evil spirit, one that causes convulsions where he became rigid, gnashed his teeth and foamed at the mouth. The evil spirit threw the boy into the fire or water repeatedly trying to kill him. Jesus released the boy and returned him to his father, well. In Luke, Chapter 6, we read an account of what appears to be a frequently occurring experience; people brought to Jesus their loved ones who were sick and afflicted by evil spirits and Jesus healed them all. Those same people if they were seen today would be given a medical or psychiatric diagnosis. The Scripture doesn't rule out illness. The accounts acknowledge there were sick people healed. But the Scripture also says plainly that there was direct spiritual attack. It causes one to wonder how often the spiritual aspect of someone's ailment is missed in the modern diagnostic process. Regardless, there are accounts of dark spiritual forces inflicting evil directly upon people.

Then Satan incites evil among us. We suffer evil at the hands of each other, with the encouragement of the evil one. *"The Devil made me do it,"* may be a cop out, but it does seem possible that he might suggest an idea, encourage it with all sorts of justifications and push someone towards a particular destructive action. We are baited, enticed and entrapped into perpetrating evil against one another. Read this from the gospel of Luke, Chapter 22:

> *[2] the chief priests and the teachers of the law were looking for some way to get rid of Jesus, for they*

*were afraid of the people. ³Then Satan entered
Judas, called Iscariot, one of the Twelve. ⁴And
Judas went to the chief priests and the officers of
the temple guard and discussed with them how he
might betray Jesus.*

Judas was a participant with evil. I don't think Judas
was possessed, or did things against his will. I think
Satan's promptings matched Judas's ambitions, and
a partnership was formed. Today, people get nudges
towards choices and behaviors that match their fleshly
drives and desires. A partnership is formed, and we
experience evil at the hands of other people.

We recognize this saying to be true, "power corrupts,
absolute power corrupts absolutely." The disclosures
of corrupt politicians and corrupt governments do
not surprise us anymore. The extent of the corruption
and the atrocities may still shock us, but the existence
of corruption is somewhat expected. Why is this
phenomenon so common that we have an expression to
describe it and we all nod our heads in acknowledgment
when we hear it? If it is simply the nature of man then
why aren't all men corrupt? Can we not recognize a
calculated plan conceived and initiated from outside
of human nature that takes advantage of the potential
for destruction in some men and women? Is it so hard
to perceive a wind at our back pushing us toward self-
destruction? It seems clear to me that Satan does incite
evil amongst us.

Satan corrupts creation so that evil becomes the natural consequence of destructive actions set in motion long ago. The old adage is true: *'hurt people hurt people.'* In case you've never heard this before and since you can't hear my inflection as you read this let me clarify. Hurt (adjective) people hurt (verb) people. As evil is perpetrated against people, the human soul is injured. There are casualties. Part of *"what is wrong with people,"* and the reason some people become perpetrators of evil, is they have first been the victims of evil. We suffer evil as a natural consequence of the evil already in the world. Satan winds up the top and sends it spinning into the world. Once under way, destruction begets destruction.

A child experiences great, great pain early in life that leaves them overwhelmed. With too little coping skills for so great a trauma, the next best alternative to managing pain is escaping it. Once escaping pain is mastered, it may remain the preferred reaction to pain even later in life when other coping skills are available. Should self-medicating progress into full-blown addiction, the process of self-medicating and the subsequent consequences produce pain for those living in relational proximity. Lies, stealing, broken commitments and the manipulation necessary to procure the next fix all cause suffering to those nearby who love and care about that person caught in addiction. If the friends and relatives have support, they may be able to manage these hurtful experiences in a healthy, functional manner. But should they be lacking support and knowledge about addiction, they may also adopt dysfunctional reactions to the pain they're experiencing. Their dysfunction creates pain for someone else who, if they respond dysfunctionally, continues the cycle. Satan has established a self-perpetuating mechanism designed to extend destruction under its own power. Satan inflicts evil upon mankind. He incites evil amongst us. He sets in motion actions whose natural consequences perpetuate evil. These are sources of damaging behavior additional to our own volition. These are the beginnings of what is wrong with people.

2

Second Impact

You know what *else* is wrong with people? After they have been wounded in the course of the battle, attempts are made to cut them off from the one source of restoration. Satan uses the pain and chaos he has created or exploited to create a barrier between people and their loving Creator. It is a common practice in warfare to use propaganda in an attempt to influence the outcome of the war. Satan is a master at using propaganda to separate people from God and His assistance.

Satan seeks to create a barrier between people and God with misinformation. Remember, Jesus called Satan *'a liar and the father of lies' (John 8:44)*. Satan will lie about the nature of God, creating an image of God that suggests God is indifferent and unloving toward us. Satan will incite us to become angry with this false image of God, until we end up taking God to task for many perceived failures on His part. If Satan can get us to entertain the thought that God might not be faithful or trustworthy, then doubt can creep into our relationship and create a barrier. If Satan can plant seeds that God might be fickle, random or even cruel, suspicion creeps in and separation from God becomes the secondary, collateral damage.

How could Satan ever pitch a believable case that God could be any of these things? He points us to the world around us, often via world news events. We see chaos, violence, systematic exploitation, neglect, famine, pandemics and injustices against the innocent and the helpless. There is childhood sexual abuse, murder, internet pornography, rampant materialism and hedonism juxtaposed against abject poverty. Even though few of us would say God is the cause of these things, the thought runs through our minds that He at least has allowed them.

The question then forms in our thinking, *"How can a good, kind, loving Father willingly permit such horrors and atrocities to happen against His supposedly beloved children?"* We imagine a moderately good, earthly father would react passionately in protection of his children, if any of these atrocities threatened their well-being. God seemingly does nothing. This question feeds other doubts, which can grow to become barriers in the heart and mind of anyone, even someone with little personal reason or desire to doubt God. We might push such doubts out of our minds, insisting they can't be true and expelling them from our consciousness, only to find the same questions sneaking back into our thoughts.

How can we combat these pesky and relentless questions? The key is this; we cannot gain a true understanding of God from our experiences in the world and our interpretations. Trying to make sense of the world around us will never result in a clear picture of who God is or what He is doing. The only true revelation of who God is and what God is like, is Jesus. When God wanted to say something about Himself, He chose carefully the word he would use to describe Himself. *Jesus* is that word. Jesus is the Word from God that reveals God.

> *¹In the beginning was the Word, and the Word was with God, and the Word was God. ²He was with God in the beginning.*
>
> *3Through him all things were made; without him nothing was made that has been made. 4In him was life, and that life was the light of men. 5The light shines in the darkness, but the darkness has not understood it.*
>
> *¹⁴The Word became flesh and made his dwelling among us. We have seen his glory, the glory of the One and Only, who came from the Father, full of grace and truth. (John 1)*

Jesus is the visible image of the invisible God as Paul writes in Colossians 1:15. Paul says, *"The Father was pleased to have His fullness dwell in Jesus."* Jesus is a full representation of God. Jesus declared this when He was correcting Phillip's lack of understanding.

> *Philip said, "Lord, show us the Father and that will be enough for us." Jesus answered, "Don't you know me, Philip, even after I have been among you*

such a long time? Anyone who has seen me has seen the Father. How can you say, 'Show us the Father'?"
John 14:8&9

So, in answer to our question, "How do I know that God is not fickle or capricious?" we find that Jesus is consistent; therefore, God is consistent. In scripture, Jesus consistently corrected self-righteous, religious types and consistently reached out to sinners. Jesus consistently showed grace before judgment. Jesus consistently showed compassion and kindness. Jesus consistently acted rightly, so much so that when his accusers were attempting to come up with charges against Jesus that they might have him executed, they could come up with nothing.

> *[57]Then some stood up and gave this false testimony against him: "We heard him say, 'I will destroy this temple made with human hands and in three days will build another, not made with hands.'" [59]Yet even then their testimony did not agree. (Mark 14)*

Keeping the above Scriptures in mind, we understand that Jesus' actions reveal the Father's heart that He is consistent, despite any confusing circumstances surrounding us

When we are watching the chaos in the news, the question comes to mind, *"What is wrong with people, and what is God doing about it?"* The answer is, God is doing as Jesus did. He is weeping for people (Luke 19:41), longing to gather to Himself those who refuse to be gathered (Matthew 23:36), reaching out repeatedly to those rejecting Him (Matthew 21:33-38), confronting evil and injustice (Luke 11:39-54, Matthew 7:5-13), all the while allowing people to walk away from Him, if that's what they choose (Matthew 19:21-22). God is giving Himself in sacrificial love in the midst of evil and chaos, just as Jesus did all these things.

With all the seemingly unexplainable incongruities we see in the world, we may be tempted to think that God's nature, character and will are mysterious. The circumstances in the world are indeed mysterious but God's nature and will are straightforward and sure, as expressed in Jesus. *God is love (1 John 4:16) and it is God's will that none should perish but all would come to repentance (2 Peter 3:9).It is God's will to seek and save what was lost (Luke 19:10). It is God's will to destroy the devil's work (1 John 3:8).* Always has been, always will be. No question.

The mystery lies in the complexity of the world we live in. Multiple cause and effect events interact, like millions of billiard balls knocking into each other on a giant pool table, altering each other's courses. One person's choice has consequences affecting those around him, making life either better or harder for him. Some people take hardship as their reason to rise above circumstance, while others use it as their justification for giving in or giving up. For example, you have influences pressing in

17

upon you all the time. These influences are the result of decisions made by other people, who were, themselves, influenced by myriads of people, who all were influenced by many people's decisions and actions. These influencing forces come from many directions all around you. They travel across the ages, from generations before you were born. Influences come from human, free-will agents, as well as spiritual forces.

These consequential and influential forces move out from choices made, much like ripples in a pool. A single action, like a pebble thrown in a pool of water, makes concentric ripples that are easy to recognize and understand. Multiple actions of varying degrees of intensity, however, create multiple ripple effects of different magnitudes; like pebbles, rocks and boulders, all being dropped into the pool at different times. The simple and easy to understand pattern of ringlets moving outward is overcome by waves crashing against each other in seemingly random ways as more and larger events occur.

If you walked upon the scene just after all the debris had been dropped into the water and only saw the effects, the various waves splashing this way and that, it would seem chaotic and arbitrary. In the same way, we look at the events in the world without seeing or knowing all the causes, and often conclude all is without rhyme or reason. Much of what is happening in the world today is the resultant wave action of many choices, made by many free-will agents, over many years and many generations. All are acting upon each other in complex combinations. We are walking in on the effects, after the causes have happened. We don't see or know all the causal agents that explain why something is happening, so it looks mysterious and without reason. There *are* reasons. We just don't know what they are. God does. We do not. As I often tell my wife, "God only knows, and He ain't telling."

This mystery bothers some people so much, they cannot, or will not, tolerate the not knowing or understanding. These people create theories and theologies in an attempt to make sense of the unknowable. In some of these theologies, God has every detail mapped out. He must, because He is all-knowing and all-powerful. God's will, therefore, cannot be thwarted or frustrated. Even terrible tragedies are part of God's will, so that a greater good can be accomplished or an important lesson can be taught.

To the young couple who has just lost a baby, one might think to offer comfort by saying, *"God needed another angel in Heaven."* To the community where a young girl is kidnapped, raped, then murdered, one might say, "Everything happens for a reason." What we might begin to feel, and what most non-Christians feel, is an irrational, weak explanation that, if true, implies that God may have a perverse and cruel strategy for interacting with the world. This impression of God, while making some sense on the surface, becomes a barrier at a deeper level.

What if, instead, God's will *can* be thwarted by people and angels with free will? Isn't this what disobedience and rebellion are, the resisting of God's will? God's ultimate desire will be accomplished, but there are a lot of specific details along the way that are left to us and to how we will choose. It is true that everything happens for a reason. Not everything happening, though, is happening for *God's* reasons. Some things happen because of Satan's reasons and purposes. Some happen because of our own. Free choice is an essential and necessary component for the world God wanted to create. He wanted to create a world where there could be love. If there is to be love in the world, then love has to be chosen. If affection is coerced, it is not love. The only way God can be loved, is if we are free to love God. The only way we are free to love God, is if we are equally free *not* to love God.

Many people have made that choice. Many people choose "not God." Many people choose selfishness, greed, indifference to others, instead of choosing godliness. Those choices thwart God's will and have consequences. God's will is not carried out when someone treats another unjustly. However, a world where people have free will choice to love or not is God's ultimate will. Spiritual beings, free will agents themselves, are waiting to exploit every choice of "not God" to further their destructive ends. They help along every bad, hurtful decision made by mortals.

What is happening is not the unfolding of a script, but the waging of a war. Evil is clashing with good, and we get caught in the crossfire. In general, bad things happen to everybody, because some free-will agents have been choosing "not God" for a long time. The consequences of those choices have been compounding, one upon the other, in more and more complex interactions. Today, it is nearly impossible to know exactly why any one specific tragedy has been thrust upon a particular person.

We *can* know this: God is not using some twisted logic and cruel means to reach some justifiable end. Evil happens, because free-will agents choose 'other than God.' God remains the same good, loving, compassionate, merciful, rescuing God. He is the God Jesus revealed when He was here on the earth. Keeping this truth clear in our minds disintegrates the barriers of misconception and misjudging God.

When we are walking through painful trials, we may feel a barrier growing as a result of our own suspicions about God's interest or love for us. There is one single event that has the power to anchor us and blast away that barrier; the crucifixion of Jesus. The crucifixion reveals that Jesus is not indifferent to our suffering in a harsh world. The crucifixion reveals Jesus was willing to enter this world and come for us. The crucifixion reveals Jesus does not perpetuate cruelty, but He does submit himself to cruelty for love's sake. The crucifixion shows God is not powerless to help us, but comes in meekness, before He comes in power. Jesus came as a lamb to be slaughtered, then was raised in power that death could not hold. Jesus works in the lives of His people, often moving in subtle ways to turn men's hearts toward God. He promises to one day come in power to gather His friends, those who endured faithfully the horrors of war, in love and loyalty to Him.

WHAT IS WRONG WITH PEOPLE?!

The truth about God revealed in Jesus blasts away barriers of accusations and slander that Satan spreads. When we help people choose this truth over deception, barriers that would keep them from God and His aid are blown away! Being clear about this important reality will give us the stamina to stay in the battle for the long haul, in the face of great opposition and sometimes seemingly small results.

Take some time to assess how your perception of God has been influenced by the events in your life. Answer honestly. How do these ideas challenge your assumptions about God or how He works in the world? What do you think about the idea that everything happens for a reason, but not always for God's reasons? If you didn't attribute the hurtful things in the world to God, how would it affect your interest and ability to draw close to Him?

Satan's strategy

I believe Satan is pedaling *three big lies* around this issue of suffering from evil, lies he hopes will drive a wedge between God and His children. They are:

1. God is not real.
2. God is not good or loving.
3. God is not powerful.

If you are a devoted follower of God then you may intuit that these questions imply things that can't possibly be true, so you dismiss them as soon as you're aware of them. But even after the mind has rejected a belief, the heart may be vexed by it if there has been life experience that seems to support it. When these lies are so quickly dismissed they can linger just outside the range of conscious thought. There, unexamined, they generate doubt that festers and grows. It is better to take a moment to evaluate what is whispered in our soul. The truth has nothing to fear from examination. It can only be confirmed as true. Lies are what seek acceptance without consideration. So, let's consider.

1. God is not real. *"How could there be a God, when the world is so out of control? This is all just random chaos, unsupervised by any deity."* I have caught myself wondering this at times. I keep coming back to one concept found in Scripture, often showing up in worship songs, this phrase, "the God of Heaven and Earth." For me, the question of whether or not God is real, is answered as I think about creation. I believe an intelligent designer is the most plausible explanation for such complex designs. Water falls from the sky as rain. It sustains plants and animals, runs through creeks to streams to rivers to lakes and oceans. From there it evaporates and begins the cycle again. Plants feed little insects and larger herbivores. Plant eaters feed meat eaters. All die, decompose and replenish the soil from which more plants grow. From ecosystems, to circulatory systems to solar systems there is consistent and intricate order. Electrons orbit nuclei as planets orbit stars. The margin of variance within which everything must operate in order for the whole to function is amazing considering the sheer number of inter-working systems there are. Under what other circumstance would an intelligent person upon discovering an unknown object with many, many, intricate moving parts wrapped in an elegant and efficiently designed cover exclaim, "Wow, what an amazing collection of random bits and pieces. How curious that they should have fallen together all on their own in such a way?" Would not an intelligent person reason that such intricate design indicates a designer? Would that person not seek out the designer for understanding about the design and purpose for such a marvelous thing so that we might extract the greatest measure of usefulness possible?

I am not satisfied with natural selection and random mutations as a reasonable explanation for things like beauty, justice, self-sacrifice, honor, mercy, forgiveness or love. These things seem contrary to a species seeking only its own survival, but very consistent with the God of the Bible. Science is a wonderful tool but a lousy substitute for God. Science for all its strength when faced with the moral, ethical, emotional and relational problems in the world has done little to deliver mankind. When a person lacks character, can science whip some up in a test tube and a beaker? God is who we instinctively look to in times of testing and crisis to make a real difference.

It is often implied that an intelligent person could not accept God as the origin of life because that is not scientific. I have wondered how it has escaped notice that the Big

Bang or spontaneous life lacks some features typically used to define the scientific method, but is still held up as the obvious rebuttal to intelligent design. I must concede that I am not a scientist. But I do remember this from the science classes I've taken. The scientific method observes phenomena and generates theories, which are then tested by experiments. Experiments control for variables so as to be able to draw accurate conclusions. Observations and experiments must be replicable so they can be corroborated or refuted by scientific peers.

As far as I'm aware, no one observed the Big Bang or the birth of life. There are no experiments that have replicated the jump from non-living to living. Even when disassembling a living cell in an environment conducive for life, no cell has ever reassembled itself and come alive. If it doesn't happen in a controlled situation with all the necessary parts readily available, what are the chances that it could happen in a primordial soup with all manner of extraneous material getting in the way and at a pace that could explain the complex interactive and interdependent world we see today? The projected life span of our sun makes it very improbable that the degree of order we see could have randomly mutated out of chaos in the time our sun's life span provides. I don't mind if that's what you choose to believe. But if you do, don't accuse me of being unintelligent or unscientific because frankly, it takes more faith to believe all of this order came together by random accident. God is the most plausible explanation for all we see.

*...since what may be known about God is plain
to them, because God has made it plain to them.
For since the creation of the world God's invisible
qualities—his eternal power and divine nature—
have been clearly seen, being understood from what
has been made, so that people are without excuse.
(Romans 1:19 &20 NIV)*

God is real. The existence of everything around us is my concrete reminder that this is true.

2. God is not good or loving. *"If God is allowing us to suffer from evil, how is that good or loving?"* Admittedly, I have also wrestled with this question. I always come back to what for me are the anchor points: greed and generosity.

I see a direct link with evil and greed; greed for power, greed for pleasure, greed for control, greed for wealth, greed for status. Greed in all its forms can be linked to most every kind of exploitation, manipulation and annihilation. The Bible says it this way:

*⁹People who want to get rich fall into temptation and
a trap and into many foolish and harmful desires
that plunge men into ruin and destruction. ¹⁰For
the love of money is a root of all kinds of evil. Some
people, eager for money, have wandered from the
faith and pierced themselves with many griefs.
(1 Timothy 6)*

¹... there will be false teachers among you. ...³In their greed these teachers will exploit you with stories they have made up....¹⁴With eyes full of adultery, they never stop sinning; they seduce the unstable; they are experts in greed—an accursed brood! (II Peter 2)

Doesn't this explanation fit your own observations and experiences? Ponzi schemes, cheating elderly people out of their meager savings, the most outrageous behavior, are so often linked to greed. The opposite seems equally true. Generosity seems to be kryptonite to evil. It's why news programs often include human interest stories of someone demonstrating exceptional kindness and generosity. It's why we watch those stories and often shed a tear. Those stories give hope and inspiration. Where there is selfless giving, good springs forth. I think of God as revealed in the Bible...

⁹This is how God showed his love among us: He sent his one and only Son into the world that we might live through him. ¹⁰This is love: not that we loved God, but that he loved us and sent his Son as an atoning sacrifice for our sins. (I John 4)
³¹What, then, shall we say in response to this? If God is for us, who can be against us? ³²He who did not spare his own Son, but gave him up for us all—how will he not also, along with him, graciously give us all things? (Romans 8)

I have experienced God as generous over and over. When I was graduating from high school, my parents divorced. As a result of the divorce, they lost everything and had to declare bankruptcy. Throughout high school I assumed I would go to college. I assumed that because that's what all of my friends were going to do. That's what you do after you've taken the college prep classes. This was a bit naive of me. No one in my family before me had ever graduated from college. I had no concept about how much college cost. I had some sense that my family and I had no money but I proceeded as though I was going to college anyway. I was reminded of this recently when the news program I was watching was describing how much debt college students graduate with today as a result of their college education. I realized that I graduated with a Bachelor of Arts degree and no debt. There was no earthly reason to think that was even possible. But it happened, through many times of favor, opportunities presented themselves. They were so many that they strained the notion of coincidence. I have other examples of God's generosity to me. Perhaps you can think of some for you too.

When life is not going as I want it to go, when there is pain and confusion, I am tempted to think that God is indifferent and uncaring. But then I remember the times that God gave to me generously. He didn't have to but He did. I didn't deserve it, but it didn't stop Him. I deserved punishment, but that's not how God treated me. I may not understand everything that God is doing in every circumstance but I am confronted with the fact that God has been generous to me. He has been divinely generous to me, giving his son to pay for my rebellion and then giving me everything else that I truly needed. Not always what I wanted, but always what I've needed. In light of such generosity, I therefore conclude God is good. God is loving.

3. God is not powerful. *"Does evil exist because God isn't strong enough to stop it?"* When considering human history, it does not appear that the church has made much progress reforming people. In many ways, it seems we are losing ground. The amount of violence in the world, the increasing depravity and decreasing conscience causes me to wonder sometimes, is this a winnable war? As I compare the obvious and dramatic effects of evil in the world to the obvious and dramatic evidence of God's activity, at least as reported in the news media, it seems discouragingly lopsided. I think this is no accident. We humans have a propensity for focusing on the negative. Satan has a propensity for exaggerating his power and denying God's. I can see Satan exploiting his strength and our weakness and offering us a method of measurement that results in declaring evil the overwhelmingly more powerful force at work in the world today. Certainly, destruction of values, prosperity and lives is all around us. If I get drawn into comparing destruction against direct divine intervention, I may reach some pessimistic conclusions. To do so however would be to miss one very important fact.

In the beginning, God created. Everything else is just a response. Only God measures His power by what He has *made and by what He can do.* Mankind measures strength by the ability to *destroy.* "Our country is stronger than your country because you guys can only destroy the world five times over and we can destroy it ten times over!" We recognize that it is far easier to tear something down than to build it. Bombs can destroy in seconds what took cultures years to build. So consider what God has built versus what Satan has built. In the creation story, God *spoke* this world into being. He didn't even have to get up out of His recliner! He didn't break a sweat! He *spoke* it into existence. What about the seventh day of *rest?* I don't think He "rested" because He was tired. I think He just wanted to admire His work. God does not faint. He does not grow weary. God is plenty powerful.

These three big lies, God is not real, God is not good, God is not powerful, play upon our fears. If people, once wounded, allow their doubts about the nature and character of God to cut them off from the one who restores, they are lost in a brokenness that compounds itself with one self-inflicted, injurious reaction after another. There is a reason the message of the New Testament is called the Gospel, literally good news.

> *[10]For if, while we were God's enemies, we were reconciled to him through the death of his Son, how much more, having been reconciled, shall we be saved through his life! (Romans 5)*

Many people still feel distant from God, even after having accepted Jesus' offer to pay for their spiritual debt. It is actually not uncommon for people to feel very excited about their spiritual awakening and their newfound friendship with Jesus in the early days of faith, only to feel like they're stalling out in their spiritual growth later. Our church participated in a study conducted by the Willow Creek Church in Chicago. This 2007 study questioned 5,000 people, from 7 different churches. The survey described four general categories of spiritual development: Exploring Christianity, Growing In Christ, Close to Christ and Christ Centered. The survey asked people to identify their current stage of growth. Survey results identified that about 16% of respondents described their present spiritual condition as being "stalled" in their spiritual growth.

For some reason, these participants had made it through the identified stages of growth, "Exploring Christianity" and "Growing in Christ", only to "Stall" before arriving "Close to Christ." Somewhere between growing in Christ and being close to Christ, a significant number of us feel like it is not quite happening. Many of us feel distant from God, even though we've made a decision to live with Him.

A Christian struggling with a sense of distance from God will often think, "There is something wrong with me." My response would be, "Well, obviously! But, it is probably not what you think."

Imagine you have a radio with a broken antenna. After running the tuner up and down the radio dial and

31

finding nothing but static, you decide there aren't any radio signals around you. In fact, the air is filled with them. The broken antenna just isn't getting any reception. People might conclude, "There is no love of God for me and no interest on His part to be near me," when, in fact, the love of God surrounds them. If our antennas are broken, we might not be getting good reception. If we have misconceptions about God and self, they act as static and keep us from perceiving the love God has for us.

This is how it happened to me. The church tradition I grew up in had a strong emphasis on right and wrong. I was taught why we were right and the other denominations were wrong. I was taught that it reflected poorly on God and my Christian witness if I were caught doing something wrong. My parents, wanting to parent correctly, reinforced the indoctrination at home. From my growing up, I developed an internal personal religious system that favored rules over relationship. I learned it in church so I assumed this was God's bias as well. My belief colored everything I read in the Bible. Somehow, all the parts that talk about Christ sufficiently satisfying the rules so relationship with Him and the Father could be opened up to me all got lost. My antenna got broken. It has taken years to be able to experience the acceptance and delight God has for me. Even though I didn't give up on God completely (as happens to many who grow weary of the rules without relationship) I felt distant from God. I did not look for God to come to my aid. I expected God to be exasperated with me and my failure. Now finally, my prayers begin with something other than an apology for being me.

This is certainly the outcome Satan seeks in waging war against God. The first wave of attack is the evil at work in the world causing pain and heartache for all of us. Then the damage is compounded by our own sinful reactions to sinful things done against us. At last, a wedge is driven between us and God. Our disappointment in God for not protecting us from all pain and our own shame at being broken keep us from drawing close to the one source of healing and restoration. Separated from the influence of God and having suffered casualties in a great, cosmic war, people can do some outrageous things. That's part of what's wrong with people.

3

Assessing The Damage

Another facet of the answer to "what is wrong with *people*," in some regard, is hiding in plain sight. People are messed up! We might hear it said, "People are fallen." In Bible terms (or Christian lingo), this means, "People have fallen from the heights of Gods original design for His creation." We are not doing as our Creator intended. If our behavior is not as He designed for us, there will be negative consequences. At the risk of being master of the obvious let me just say, sin has negative consequences.

God did not arbitrarily pick some things to be '*sin*' and others to be '*righteousness*.' Some people presume He decided, "Anything fun is sin, and anything hard or tedious is righteousness." Rather, the truth is that everything in line with God's nature and character is righteousness and, therefore, life-giving. In the same way, everything outside of God's nature is sin, and, therefore, harmful. God does not tell us not to sin so we can be morally superior. God tells us not to sin to keep us from hurting ourselves and those around us.

Here is something else to consider. "Other people's sin can have negative impact on me." Part of what is wrong with me is the result of sinful choices I have made and the resulting consequences. But some of what is wrong with me is the consequence of someone else's sinful choice. Someone chose to do something hurtful. I didn't get a vote. They just decided to do it. Though I had no say in their decision, I am still negatively affected. I often complicate matters by having a sinful reaction to the sin done against me. Both have a negative effect on my condition. It can get complicated, very quickly. The end result is that I am messed up. I am no longer, in action or condition, as God designed me.

In searching for the answer to "what is wrong with people?", there is another interesting twist. There can actually be four things wrong with us. What is more, any of the four may happen in combination with each other in varying degrees. If you do the math, it adds up to a lot of possible combinations. These are the four specific things that can go wrong with people:

Injury
Immaturity
Habits
Oppression

Injury

Injury is most common in our emotions and our memories of past events. Actions done against us of a violent, neglectful or disrespectful nature can be wounding to our souls. Besides whatever physical harm that may have happened, there can be an associated injury to our sense of identity and worth. People who have been abused at early ages sometimes believe they deserve to be abused. They accept, and possibly even seek out abuse, being hurt over and over again, deepening and reinforcing the original wound.

The emotional pain of such trauma can be overwhelming when it happens to us before we have had the chance to develop sufficient coping skills. This pain often gets warehoused in our deep-heart, emotional storage. Locked away out of sight, it can cause infection. The outcome might be bitterness, rage and a lack of trust—all of which may have been appropriate responses to the original offense. Once internalized, these infected responses become the filter through which we view and respond to the world. It is like having little monsters painted on the lenses of our eyeglasses. Everywhere we look, we see big monsters. Projecting the pain and injury outward can impair our relationships. Circumstances that are even slightly similar to our past memories can trigger all the pain associated with those memories and cause us to react as if the original injury was happening all over again.

This deep-heart infection can affect any/all of our relationships, but especially our relationship with God. Have you ever seen someone who was hypersensitive and over-reactive to the least of slights? If so, you have probably met someone with deep hurt. Have you ever wondered, "Why do they act like that?" If so, know this: they probably ask themselves the same question. In fact, their question is likely more harsh, such as, "Why do I keep doing this over and over?" When there is an injury hiding in the deep-heart storage, undetected, untreated and operating undeterred by any rational thought or evaluation, infected behavior and beliefs flourish.

Immaturity

In seeking to understand how immaturity is part of what is wrong with people, let's consider some hallmarks of maturity/immaturity. Look at the comparison chart below:

Mature	Immature
Impulse control	Impulsive
Can delay gratification	Insists on immediate gratification
Can experience legitimate pain for a greater good	Avoids/medicates all pain
Can grasp paradox	All or nothing/black & white thinking
Owns mistakes	Blames others
Makes amends	Makes excuses
Thoughtfully responds	Emotionally reacts
Sharing	Consuming
Expresses the full range of emotions	Emotionally closed or explosive
Able to take direction and input	Willfully independent, closed to correction
Can live and work within limits of appropriate authority	Tests limits reflexively

It's important to realize that immaturity may not be the fault of the individual. There are some things you would only know or be able to do because someone taught you. If there was no one there to teach you those things, you would not have developed them. It may not be a person's *fault* that they are not fully mature in some aspects of his life, but it is still his *responsibility*. A childish adult is still childish. It doesn't matter whose fault it is, it's still a problem.

> [11]*When I was a child, I talked like a child, I thought like a child, I reasoned like a child. When I became a man, I put childish ways behind me. (1 Corinthians 13)*

Childish impulses and childish perspectives can interfere with our experience of God and our success in living. It is true Jesus said, "*Unless you receive the kingdom of God like a little child you cannot enter it.*" *(Matthew 18:3)* Here, Jesus is referring to the humility and trusting abandonment in which little children live. This is the same kind of trust we are to retain or possibly rediscover, while still being adults.

The writer of Hebrews wrote in Chapter 5:11-14,

> *We have much to say about this, but it is hard to explain because you are slow to learn. In fact, though by this time you ought to be teachers, you need someone to teach you the elementary truths*

*of God's word all over again. You need milk, not
solid food! Anyone who lives on milk, being still an
infant, is not acquainted with the teaching about
righteousness. But solid food is for the mature,
who by constant use have trained themselves to
distinguish good from evil.*

The writer calls out an immaturity among those people that was preventing them from understanding and experiencing all they could be experiencing. Kids do not understand why they need to eat their vegetables, go to bed at a reasonable hour, not hit their brothers and sisters and do their homework. They don't do these things naturally, but must be trained. We may know adults who still struggle with eating right, getting enough rest, playing well with others or carrying out their responsibilities. We may be those adults!

Until children *do* learn these responsibilities, certain privileges might be withheld, such as driving the family car or having a later curfew. Ideally, children learn that privileges come with being responsible, and being responsible earns privileges. Again, we all know people in adult-sized bodies who still have not learned these things, and who go through life with a sense of entitlement matched with irresponsibility.

Spiritually speaking, when we are young in our faith, it is hard to grasp why we should tithe 10% of our income, give our time to service of others who cannot repay us or understand why God would ask us to sacrifice or suffer.

Immaturity might have us expecting that God should be all about blessing us and making us happy, even while we ignore much of what He has to say about how we are to live. The angry, frustrated child who yells at their parents, *"You don't love me! You never want me to have any fun!,"* is the voice of immaturity. And immaturity can cause people to cry out to God, *"You are not really good. You don't truly love me!"* A barrier then grows between us and God, because He is failing to deliver on our childish expectations. If we give into the temptation to pout until we get our way, we can really cement a barrier between us and God. The person who fails to mature and master the abilities associated with maturity will struggle in life. If the frustration that can come with immaturity is directed at God, the problem is compounded. That frustration can drive a wedge between us and the one who can and wants to grow us up.

Habits

What do you think of when you think of "bad habits?" Some might be chewing with your mouth open, belching in public, smoking, biting your fingernails, texting while driving, etc. We identify bad habits as behaviors that are detrimental to us in some way, ways we have been unable to stop. Addictions are the ultimate in bad habits. Addictions are bad habits on steroids! They are a little more complicated than simple bad habits, as they may have a physiological dependency, but you get the point.

In addition to having behavioral bad habits, we can also have bad thought habits. Pessimism is when we become habituated to expecting the worst. A critical nature is when we become habituated to being judgmental of others. Arrogance is the mental habit of thinking of ourselves as being more important than others.

We can also become habituated to emotions. Some people fly into a rage whenever their wants are frustrated. Regardless, something big or small, the same raging response is elicited. There was a time when I was depressed. After therapy, a lot of renewing my mind and some anti-depressant medication, the hold of my depression was broken. Shortly after, something happened that made me sad. Except, I didn't stop at sad. I began to slip into depression again. This time, I caught it! I reminded myself that just because I always felt that way before, did not mean I had to feel that way again. I had new options available to me now. It took effort and the use of some new coping tools not to fall back into the familiar habit of feeling depressed.

Oppression

Spiritual oppression can be an intimidating thought that conjures up images from the movie, "The Exorcist." Here, we are not talking about exorcisms and demonic possession. We are not talking about spiritual boogey men taking over the will and body of a person. We *are* talking about spiritual beings who are real, who are described in the Bible as having interactions with people—even if that seems outside the norm of western thought. In the Gospels, most of the accounts of evil spirits describe Jesus casting demons out of people. Why, then, are we *not* talking about demon possession?

Jesus told his disciples in John 16:5-7,

> *"Now I am going to him who sent me, yet none of you asks me, 'Where are you going?' Because I have said these things, you are filled with grief. But I tell you the truth: It is for your good that I am going away. Unless I go away, the Counselor will not come to you; but if I go, I will send him to you."*

And in Luke 24:49,

> *"I am going to send you what my Father has promised; but stay in the city until you have been clothed with power from on high."*

At the time Jesus was casting out demons from people, His Spirit had not yet been sent to live in the hearts of people. After Jesus ascended to Heaven, the Holy Spirit fell on the disciples at Pentecost. The Holy Spirit came to the gentile Cornelius and his household. The prophecy came true:

> *"I will pour out my Spirit on all people. Your sons and daughters will prophesy, your old men will*

dream dreams, your young men will see visions. Even on my servants, both men and women, I will pour out my Spirit in those days."(Joel 2:28 & 29)

Those who have accepted Christ as Lord and invited the Spirit of God to live in them, do indeed have the Spirit of God in them. In 2 Corinthians 6:14-15, Paul writes,

Do not be yoked together with unbelievers. For what do righteousness and wickedness have in common? Or what fellowship can light have with darkness? What harmony is there between Christ and Belial? What does a believer have in common with an unbeliever?

Darkness cannot have fellowship or coexist with God's light. We therefore conclude that, with the Holy Spirit living within us, it would be intolerable for an evil spirit to take up residence in us.

John gives us his testimony in 1 John 4:1-4,

Dear friends, do not believe every spirit, but test the spirits to see whether they are from God, because many false prophets have gone out into the world. This is how you can recognize the Spirit of God: Every spirit that acknowledges that Jesus Christ has come in the flesh is from God, but every spirit that does not acknowledge Jesus is not from God. This is the spirit of the antichrist, which you have heard is coming and even now is already in the world.

You, dear children, are from God and have overcome them, because the one who is in you is greater than the one who is in the world.

The Spirit of God is in you. He is greater than the evil one in the world. Therefore, evil spirits *cannot* take possession of a Spirit-filled Christ follower and exercise control from within. I *do* believe, however, that a Spirit-filled Christ follower can be harassed or oppressed from without by evil spirits. It is this oppression that can lead people to do incredibly destructive things. If we revisit our broken antenna analogy, oppression is like un-welcomed static that interferes with clear reception of God's love and power. Not to fear, because Jesus said in Luke 4 that He came to release the oppressed.

What would oppression look like? Emotionally, we may find heavy moods settle on us, perhaps in conjunction with an unfortunate event or randomly, with no obvious cause. What if you do all the things *'you are supposed to do'* when that happens (i.e., go to counseling, forgive those who have hurt you, take anti-depressant medicines under a doctor's supervision), yet we are still feeling deep sadness, fear or confusion? If this is the case, there may be a spiritual force with its finger tipping the scale.

Intellectually, we may have oppressive and intrusive thoughts constantly bombarding our minds. It is often assumed by people,' If a thought is in my mind, then it must be my thought.' Not always true. When you are reading a book, the author puts his thoughts in your mind as you read his words. You then have to decide if you agree or disagree and whether you will embrace or reject the thought. Spirits interject thoughts that do not originate within us. We must discern, "Are these thoughts from God? Are they from the evil one? Are they possibly my own thoughts?" God's thoughts, I accept. Satan's thoughts, I reject. My thoughts, I scrutinize for accuracy. We must push back the lies and hold fast to the truth.

Relationally, have you ever been at odds with someone, and you can't figure out why? Have you ever felt like you wanted to be mad at someone, but had no good reason? I believe we get nudges toward behavior that can cause breaches in our relationships with each other and definitely with God. Relentless nudges in that direction could be described as oppression.

Now, reflect on your own experiences. Can you recognize places in your own soul that have been injured? Do you still carry hurts from long ago? Can you think of the ways you had no one to nurture you regarding some important character trait or life ability? Do you remember the attempts you made to teach yourself, to in effect raise yourself? At the mention of behavioral, mental and emotional habits, do some of yours come right to mind? Do you recall promises you've made to yourself over and over again only to break them, over and over again? Have you ever had the experience that, no matter how hard you tried to correct some flaw or fault of yours, there seemed to be some invisible force opposing you, preventing progress? If you resonate with any or all of these phenomena, you will have to modify a universal question.

The title of this book is, "What is *wrong* with people!?" When we ask this question, what we really mean is, "What is wrong with *those* people?!" If we measure our experiences against what I have presented here and find any commonality, we will have to begin to ask instead, "What is wrong with *us* people?!" In humility, we have to admit that we, too, have been affected and influenced. We, too, are capable of saying and doing ridiculous and hurtful things. We are all in a similar predicament. Should we be successful at tempering our frustration and outrage with honest humility, we may find we have greater patience and greater compassion for one another.

We may also learn to address what is in our own hearts, before we get too worked up about what other people are doing. If we have any inclination to evaluate someone else or any intention of helping another, we must first assess the condition of our own soul. We cannot judge someone for the speck in their eye when we have a board in our own, without being a hypocrite. We cannot hope to lead someone else where we have not gone. We cannot give away what we do not ourselves possess. In order to have any positive influence on the people around us, we must first conduct that fearless moral inventory and ask God, *"Search my heart and see if there be any wounded, stunted, stuck or wicked way in me." (Psalm 139:23-24)*

47

4

For Injury, There is Healing

Injuries to our spirits and our souls *require* healing. Without a healing touch, no amount of moral instruction, determination or intentionality will ever correct the sinful behavior resulting from injuries suffered. This is true for both injuries received at the hands of others, as well as those self-inflicted by our own sinful choices. In the Growth and Healing Ministry at our church, we continue to watch and learn God's design for healing. Our observation of His process goes something like this:

1. Taking inventory– discovering the forgotten, repressed, denied pieces
2. Bringing it into the light– sharing with safe people, experiencing loving reactions
3. Expression of emotions– giving voice to anger, grief, hopelessness, sorrow
4. Release and forgiveness– beginning the process that sets us free from the past
5. Invite Jesus to begin the Healing of memories

and emotions—doing for us what we cannot do
for ourselves

6. Plan for the future– learning from the past what
    part I can play to have a better future

Healing Step 1

Taking inventory — discovering the forgotten, repressed,
denied pieces.

Taking inventory is best and most easily done in
a safe environment. Trustworthy people; counselors,
support groups and healthy friends are valuable for
creating the safety necessary to go to the recesses of
old memories to get in touch with experiences long forgotten. The presence of safe people makes it possible to
open hearts and minds, to invite Jesus to reveal what
has been hidden. He is merciful to reveal only those
things one can bear to know. Jesus is perfect in His
timing, knowing which hurts *need* to be revealed, and
in what order. Patterns of unpleasant emotions or dysfunctional behavior being repeated in one's life may offer clues to what is hiding in the deep heart. The Holy
Spirit knows how to guide us to what is next in this
journey of healing.

Often, the insights come as we have opportunity
to talk through the past with our chosen "safe" person.
The critical piece for us, is to be willing to trust the Holy
Spirit; willing to know what we have been invested in not
knowing for a long time. There may need to be a shift in

our priorities to allow us to do this work. Some aspects of physical healing have pain associated with them, such as injections or surgery. We submit to *that* pain for the sake of greater healing. If we have experienced multiple or severe emotional injuries, we may have made an inner vow never to allow ourselves to feel that kind of pain again. We will now need to recommit from pain avoidance to healing.

Remembering the past can threaten to be unbearable. But unaddressed injury and its results can be excruciating. Our situation can become further complicated if we do not connect the cause and the effect and make needed changes. Things may *feel* worse before they *get* better. What we are trading is pain with no hope of getting better in exchange for pain with the hope of healing. This is not pain for pain's sake, but pain for healing's sake.

This deep cleansing can be difficult and tempting to avoid. Like a wound, one can either pull off the scab and put on a Band-Aid, or go deeper, inviting God to remove all of the infection and allowing the healing process to begin. The more thoroughness at this stage, the more healing will happen. Sometimes folks will underestimate the extent of their wounding. Believing they are finished with their process, they may stop their work just short of God's completion of their journey of healing. In His merciful thoroughness, He will bring them back to this same injury, over and over, until they have fought through and their healing is complete.

Healing Step 2

Bringing it into the light — sharing with safe people, experiencing loving reactions.

Our *minds* can be changed with persuasive evidence and compelling arguments. To convince our *hearts* of something new, we need emotionally corrective *experiences*. If our memory recalls times we were mistreated, how is our heart to know that mistreatment was not what we deserved? What are required are new, redemptive experiences of compassion, caring and love. Our typical expectation is, "If anyone finds out about my past, they'll despise me, pity me and reject me." Our heart sometimes believes this kind of reaction is what we deserve because of what we have been through. Why else would it have happened in the first place, if we didn't do something to deserve it? What if we do get the courage to risk sharing our painful secrets with another person and that person does not act in any of those hurtful ways? What if, instead, people treated us with respect, dignity and caring when we opened up about our imperfections? Imagine how healing that experience is to the human heart!

Things hiding in the dark lose their power to bully us when brought into the light. When you were a child lying in your darkened bedroom, the shirt draped over a chair across the room looked like a monster about to eat you! In the light, it turned back into a shirt on a chair. Our personal painful histories and their memories hiding in the darkness of our deep heart threaten us. Those memories seem to be insurmountable, invincible monsters that will haunt us and rule us for life. When brought into the light of knowing and being known, they are revealed as truly painful bits of the past, not the monsters we have imagined.

Uncovering these heartaches and inviting the light to shine upon them can be the scariest piece of the healing puzzle. It can also bring an incredible amount of healing. This process works, not only when we have been sinned against, but also when we have reacted to our own hurts in sinful ways. Bringing our injuries and sinful reactions into the light helps uncover the shame and breaks the power of the sin.

Giving voice and expression to the injury takes it out of the realm of the mind. To declare, "Yes, this really did happen and it really did hurt" is powerful. Most importantly, the person chosen to share this time of vulnerability with us must be safe and completely trustworthy. God may draw the wounded into deep heart discovery and even confession, confession able to facilitate great healing. There must be a clear sense of confidentiality and safety present before approaching the sanctuary of any heart, much less one deeply wounded. If the injury is deep enough, this could be a time when someone with professional level knowledge and skills will be helpful. If the occasion arises where you are honored to be the hearer of someone's confessions, it is wise to know when you have done the part that is within your ability as a friend and when it is time to find someone more equipped for this part of the healing process.

Healing Step 3

Expression of emotions — anger, grief, hopelessness, sorrow, joy, fear, confusion

All emotions deserve a voice, not just the pleasant ones. Emotions that have *not* been given a voice typically don't go away. They simply accumulate. If enough emotions awaiting expression build up, they can reach critical mass. Should this happen, the slightest of triggers can release them in an explosion. This is usually a very messy affair, leaving you embarrassed, and your friends wondering, "Where did that come from?" Though the emotions expressed may be related to the event that set them off, they are, obviously, overboard in comparison to the trigger.

An example: Someone says something that is a little abrasive or someone cuts into line in front of you. Inexplicably, you erupt into a long and loud rant about rudeness being rampant in society, how common courtesy *must* be restored, and you aren't going to take it anymore! Repressed emotions can lead to explosive emotional outbursts.

The guideline we use in our Growth & Healing ministry, is to express emotions in ways that won't hurt ourselves, other people, or property that doesn't belong to us (or that we will regret losing later). Our Divorce and Beyond ministry has an anger party where they throw dishes representing the wrongs done against them. This can be very cathartic. They are not destroying someone else's dishes, and they are not destroying the china their grandmother left them! Sometimes these folks go out into a field or the woods and scream; they do not scream in someone's face! Other times they write out their emotions on a slip of paper and burn it in a fireplace; they don't set fire to someone's house (with the person in it)!

There are many creative ways to express emotion; drawing, painting, writing, running, crying. Less creative perhaps, but still effective: using words to express our emotions.

At times, it is helpful to express emotions with the person who is the catalyst for those emotions. Sometimes it works to share our feelings with a caring friend who was not involved in the source of the emotion. Other times, it is enough just to tell Jesus. The emotion may even be blocking our experience with Him and getting it out can open up connectivity again.

Healing Step 4

Release and forgiveness — a process that sets us free from the past

We might get a lump in our throat and a knot in our stomach just thinking about forgiving some of the things people have done to us. Such reactions come from the size and traumatic nature of the injury and from our own misunderstandings around forgiveness.

What forgiveness is <u>not</u>...

Forgiveness is <u>not</u> a feeling. We do not need to have warm fuzzy feelings about the people we are forgiving. Some of them may actually be dangerous, malicious and totally without remorse. It can be hard to have happy feelings when thinking about them or what they have done to us.

The memory of what has happened to us may continue to produce painful feelings for a while. If someone steps on your toe and then apologizes, you can choose to forgive him. It is likely your toe will still hurt. The apology does not make your toe stop hurting immediately. Some of the injuries we have suffered are just going to hurt for a while, even after we choose to forgive. Persistent, painful feelings do not mean that we were insincere or ineffective in forgiving. Those feelings do not have to stop us from beginning to forgive.

Forgiveness is <u>not</u> denial. When someone asks for forgiveness, we might say, "That's OK," but the truth is it's not OK! It is not all right for people to hurt each other. A better response is, "I forgive you." Somehow, these words hold power and are good to hear. It lets the forgiven person know that our desire is to wipe the slate clean. It is good to say, because it acknowledges the wrong and also exercises our will to choose to release it. Just saying "That's OK," avoids both.

In fact, we can only forgive to the extent that we have taken inventory of the wrong done against us. If when offering forgiveness we minimize a great wound, we only release the little bit of the wrong being acknowledged. The rest stays around haunting us with pain, bitterness and resentment. People sometimes wonder why they still have so much pain, even after they have attempted to forgive someone. It might be they have minimized the amount of injustice done against them. Only when we say, "This is the full extent of the injustice done to me. This is the full impact it has had on my life. I forgive you," do we have a shot at getting free of the whole measure of past pain.

Forgiveness is <u>not</u> reconciliation. As we mentioned before, the person who hurt us may still be committed to doing hurtful actions. If so, we can release them from what they have done to us in the past. We must then remove ourselves from further relationship with them, to avoid incurring more injury in the future. In fact, cutting off the relationship may be necessary, not optional. Giving forgiveness is not the same as granting permission to keep hurting us again and again. As a result of forgiveness, we might regard someone as being clean in our relationship currently. But we may also need to steer clear of that person until he changes his ways.

I had a person in my life with whom I shared both a close and conflictual relationship. There was genuine caring between us from the beginning. There was also a pattern of interaction that caused us both a great deal of pain. This person had grown up with a strong demanding father. It is my guess that if he had preferences that differed from his father's that they were dismissed or even rebuked. What was more clear was that in our relationship he struggled to ask for his personal preferences. If he had, he could have gotten much of what he wanted. Instead, in his thinking, he transformed his personal preferences into universally accepted and known values. This made it possible for him to think he could expect to get what he wanted and needed. But because he viewed them as being universally known, he did not express them, at least not until they were not met. Then, when his preferences were not met, he would harbor pain as that of being victimized. Still being reluctant to speak up for himself, he would hold onto the pain until it grew with repeated failures to anticipate and deliver his wants. It would grow until the point that it was too great to hold in.

At that time, he would "hold a boundary" which was usually a unilateral decision about how our relationship would go that was enforced upon me. It was intended to protect him but it often caused pain in me both by nature of whatever boundary/punishment was devised but also because it branded me as the perpetrator of the victimization. The repeated "villainization" of me and my character brought me to the place that I could no longer stay in the relationship. When we parted ways, it was ugly.

Some time passed and that person reached out to me in a gesture to reconnect. I was apprehensive about the meeting. The pain was still clear in my memory. But I knew that it was the right thing to do to at least be open to reconciling. So I agreed to meet. He extended the olive branch in the context that he had heard God say to him that in the time that had passed I had grown. I was no longer the person he remembered me to be and so he wanted to get to know the new me. I found the conversation awkward but gave it my best. I was able to say that in the time since our break in relationship God had persuaded me that he was a good person and that the dysfunctions we each had were just the right kind so as to trigger one another repeatedly. I expressed that our slate was clean as far as I was concerned. I had the impression that there was the intention on his part that this would restore our interaction and relationship. I felt like something still wasn't right.

It wasn't until I had some time to think about the conversation that I was able to put my finger on what felt off to me. The idea that I had grown and wasn't the person he remembered was intended as an offer of mercy and grace. However, it didn't quite hit me that way. Then I made the connection. Not only was I not the person today that he remembered. I wasn't that person he remembered even back then. It is my belief that his memory was distorted by his lack of confidence to own and ask for what he wanted. He distorted his preferences into inalienable rights and made me the great transgressor of what was good and appropriate. I am persuaded that unless he comes to grips with the hurts within himself and the results of that pain on his thinking and behavior we are likely to repeat the same pattern of behavior we once practiced. We would most probably pick up where we left off hurting each other. I forgave him for the past hurts and I chose not to reestablish relationship. Forgiveness is not the same as reconciliation.

What forgiveness is...

Forgiveness is a decision; a decision to relinquish our right to retaliation, putting the responsibility for bringing justice into God's hands.

In Psalm 89, we read...

> *13 Your arm is endowed with power; your hand is strong, your right hand exalted. 14 Righteousness and justice are the foundation of your throne; love and faithfulness go before you. (NIV)*

The writer affirms God as the source of true justice, uncompromised by any sinful corruption, fully capable. And so the Apostle Paul advises us in Romans Chapter 12

> *19Do not take revenge, my friends, but leave room for God's wrath, for it is written: "It is mine to avenge; I will repay," says the Lord. (NIV)*

Forgiveness is the decision to turn over the task of seeking justice to the One who is qualified and competent to be just. This does not mean we must insulate people from the natural consequences of their wrong behaviors, including legal penalties. But it does call us to relinquish our internal sense of moral obligation.

Forgiveness is canceling the debt. From an early age, we instinctively recognize the indebtedness of being wronged or wronging another. What if we suffer, even a small slight, at the expense of another? What if this small slight is even among friends, even in jest? We might say, "You *owe* me now!" We speak of paying our debt to society. One symbol of justice is a blindfolded woman holding a scale. The blindfold represents impartiality. The scale was used to weigh the precious metal being used as currency, often gold or silver, to the exact measure of the purchase price required. We sense, in the core of our being, a wrong committed equals indebtedness.

Forgiveness *is* writing off the moral debt someone owes us. When that person wronged us, he went in the red on our relational ledger. Forgiveness wipes the slate clean. We no longer have anything to hold over his head. We surrender our leverage to make him feel bad or obligated to us. We relinquish the power that comes from holding the moral high ground. We give up our superiority and declare that we both are on even ground.

Forgiveness is a process. "I decided yesterday. I decide today. If you ask me tomorrow, my decision will remain the same"

Small slights among friends we know really love us can probably be forgiven in a moment. Grievous wounds are not resolved so quickly. Like a big mound of horse manure dumped in our yard, we may have to get rid of it one shovel full at a time.

61

One might think the first step in the process of forgiving is to become willing to forgive. In some instances, the evil committed and the pain caused has been so great, that realistically there may be one step before that. I have often had to pray the prayer, "God make me willing *to become* willing to forgive." I have found God to be very gracious and accommodating with even such a modest amount of submission.

Even this step of becoming willing to forgive may take some time to unfold. It usually entails an increased understanding on our part, about the one who has wronged us. He is a person, not a monster. He is likely a victim, as well as a perpetrator. Out of his wounds he has wounded. We use a familiar expression, "Hurt people, hurt people." This does not excuse what has been done to us, though it may explain part of it. At the point we can see our offender as human, we can relate to him. We are clearly aware of the harm done against us. But what if the injuries and experiences in his life leading up to this offense had happened to us? Could we, would we have done any better? When we choose to pause and reflect in this way, we typically will find ourselves becoming a little more willing to consider forgiving.

Often, though, we find ourselves dragging our feet, with objection after objection, resisting the call to forgive. The most frequently used strategy for avoiding forgiving is to put conditions on our forgiveness of others:

- When they admit they are wrong...
- If they ask for forgiveness...

- When they have suffered equally to our suffering...
- If they promise to never do it again...

THEN, we will forgive.

Here's what is so attractive to me about these conditions. These conditions *seem* to get me off the hook, because the people I am having the most trouble forgiving will likely never choose to meet any of them! Unfortunately for my unforgiving tendencies, only one true condition for forgiveness is endorsed in Scripture. I must forgive others because of my condition. I am a person standing in need of forgiveness myself and the moral debt anyone could owe me is far smaller than the debt I owe to my creator.

Jesus told a parable in Matthew Chapter 18 to make this point very clear.

> *21Then Peter came to Jesus and asked, "Lord, how many times shall I forgive my brother when he sins against me? Up to seven times?"*
>
> *22Jesus answered, "I tell you, not seven times, but seventy-seven times.*
>
> *23"Therefore, the kingdom of heaven is like a king who wanted to settle accounts with his servants. 24As he began the settlement, a man who owed him ten thousand talents was brought to him. 25Since he was not able to pay, the master ordered that he and his wife and his children and all that he had be sold to repay the debt.*

26"The servant fell on his knees before him. 'Be patient with me,' he begged, 'and I will pay back everything.' 27The servant's master took pity on him, canceled the debt and let him go.

28"But when that servant went out, he found one of his fellow servants who owed him a hundred denarii. He grabbed him and began to choke him. 'Pay back what you owe me!' he demanded.

29"His fellow servant fell to his knees and begged him, 'Be patient with me, and I will pay you back.'

30"But he refused. Instead, he went off and had the man thrown into prison until he could pay the debt. 31When the other servants saw what had happened, they were greatly distressed and went and told their master everything that had happened.

32"Then the master called the servant in. 'You wicked servant,' he said, 'I canceled all that debt of yours because you begged me to. 33Shouldn't you have had mercy on your fellow servant just as I had on you?' 34In anger his master turned him over to the jailers to be tortured, until he should pay back all he owed.

35"This is how my heavenly Father will treat each of you unless you forgive your brother from your heart." (NIV)

Reading and understanding this parable challenges me. I can only say, "On the condition that I need and want forgiveness for my greater debt with God, I willingly release you from your relatively smaller debt with me." This works for every heinous evil that one human could inflict upon another, if you consider that on the other side of the scale is every sin of commission and omission I have ever committed from the day of my birth until now. Every deed, word and thought that proceeded from my self-centered, self-absorbed, greedy, lustful, envious, ungrateful, jealous, raging, disrespecting, insulting, slanderous flesh goes against the wrong this one person has done to me. What if someone is given to minimizing his sin by comparison with others? *"I am not as bad as THAT guy!"* Even that person must concede that merely by accumulation over time, the amount of his own debt has to be staggering. I find that for myself it is only getting worse as the years (now numerous) pass by. God's call to forgiveness is relentless and without loopholes.

In light of that fact, let me cut you a little slack. Remember we said earlier, forgiveness is not the same as reconciliation? In reconciliation you can have stricter conditions, such as: requiring the person to take ownership of their actions, to make restitution, to seek help to change a broken heart condition, to make a plan and a commitment to change how they treat me in the future. All these are valid requirements for the restoration and resuming of a relationship. Just be aware that these conditions can slip into becoming barriers and excuses for unforgiveness. The pressing nature of God's call to forgive is more easily endured when you realize the answer to one little trick question...

Who benefits from forgiveness? When God offers forgiveness, it is to the benefit of the forgiven.

When I extend my forgiveness, it is primarily for the benefit of the forgiver, me. When I hang on to unforgiveness, I am the one burdened by carrying around the baggage of the past. I am the one living with past pain, because I keep feeding it with my unforgiveness and keep it alive. I am the one who suffers. Not forgiving someone is like drinking in the poison of bitterness and resentment and thinking it will make *them* sick.

God's call to forgive mean, remorseless people, is not a cruel trick that adds one more injustice on top of all the others. His call to forgiveness is the antidote for a deadly disease of the heart and spirit. This disease always ends the same; death, in slow, agonizing degrees. Forgiving is perhaps the most critical part of the process of healing.

Healing Step 5

Invite Jesus to begin the Healing of memories and emotions. If we do only the helping skills described in this book, we end up doing little more than what any secular counseling or social service agency can do. We, however, have access to a supreme force. I say, "Let's cheat!" Let's be intentional about asking the creator and sustainer of the universe for His input and intervention. God is the source of all healing. We are remiss if we do not approach Him for his power. We need God to do for us, what we cannot do for ourselves.

We have used a prayer model in our ministry known as 'Theophostic Prayer' (www.theophostic.com). In my early days of counseling, we used something similar called 'Guided Imagery.' Unlike secular counseling, we did not attempt to guide the imagination. We asked the Holy Spirit to do so. 'Theophostic Prayer' has developed a process for leading a person to invite Jesus to join them in their memories of past hurts. They specifically ask Him to tell them whatever He has to say about them or their experiences. Those of us who have participated in this prayer, have been amazed at what gets revealed. We can only conclude that we are, in fact, getting divine help.

We want to be alert to managing expectations. Once people pray, they sometimes assume the ball is now in God's court, and it is up to Him to resolve all that is wrong. The reality instead is prayer has engaged God in a partnership with people. In this partnership, God certainly will do for us what we cannot do for ourselves. He also seems inclined to give people assignments, such as remembering, repenting and forgiving.

A normal response might be reluctance, if not defiance, about *not* doing our part. We may keep returning for more prayer. If we did not experience a supernatural response from God the first time, we might seek out "more potent prayer warriors because the last ones did not get the job done! We have seen God be patient and persistent in His insistence that there are some things *we* must do, and He will not do those for us. Under the best of circumstances, the responsibility for the next action step goes back and forth. God asks us to do something, then, He does something. He gives us the next piece for us to do, after which He is free to do His next part. It is surprising to some people that God expects them to do some work. We have to help them adjust their expectations. This also means that the healing they seek may not be instantaneous, but a process that works itself out over time, in stages of progress. This can be disappointing to the person who was hoping for a quick fix. Let's be honest, isn't quick and painless what we all hope for? We may need to educate people about how God tends to work and encourage them to remain faithful, hopeful and active in their healing.

Healing Step 6

Plan for the future — discovering what part I can play to learn from the past and have a better future.

As we help people recover from past hurts, there are two areas we need to help them address to increase hope that being hurt like this in the future is less likely. The first is learning to recognize and avoid dangerous situations or people. Often people's early emotional and spiritual injuries occur when they are quite vulnerable. When we are young, we are trusting of adults. We believe they are right, wise and looking out for our best interests. Sadly, this is not always the case. As we grow older, and especially when we become adults, we learn that adults can be wrong, immature and wounded. Their actions come out of these conditions. There are adults, who, because of their own wounding, have become predatory, looking for vulnerable victims to satisfy their own aching longings in sinful and dysfunctional ways.

We must learn the skill of discernment. We must learn to recognize signs that someone might be out to harm us. One clue is when a new acquaintance is being overly generous or flattering. Someone who caters to our every desire and joins us in blaming the whole rest of the world for not understanding us or caring about us as we think we deserve, could be up to something. They may be planning to swarm us with attention and affirmation, gaining unquestioning trust, without our actually knowing anything about the individual. Behaviors like these play on our valid feelings and needs in an overly exuberant way.

We must learn how to trust people in responsible ways. Trust is earned when people show themselves to be trustworthy, consistently, over time. People who insist we trust them when we barely know them, who feign being insulted by caution on our part are probably running some kind of game. We must learn to trust new relationships with little matters first, and see how we are treated. When people show respect and regard for us and what matters to us, we can begin to risk some of our more precious treasure, our deeper thoughts, feelings, hopes, dreams and concerns.

Discernment helps us live between naiveté and paranoia. When we have developed sufficient skills of discernment, we will stop giving away our trust and treasures to people who have not earned such a right. Neither will we live in fear and constant suspicion of every person we meet. We will stop requiring that people be perfect and never disappoint us, before we open up to them. No one will be perfect, not even our best friends. In time, we learn that perfection is not necessary. It will be enough if, when someone hurts or disappoints us, they take ownership for their actions without excuse, show true remorse and make a commitment to do better by us in the future.

The skill of discernment is important and often underdeveloped in many people. At our church, we regularly do support groups to assist folks in gaining this ability. In these groups, we use the book Safe People by Henry Cloud and John Townsend (Zondervan), and have seen good results. Mentioning the good Doctors Cloud and Townsend reminds me of another of their books we use to help people in this area (We actually use just about everything they have written. It's all good stuff!). We offer support groups that last around 12 weeks using the book Boundaries, to help people gain proficiency at setting and holding boundaries.

Some potentially dangerous people can't be avoided altogether. They may be co-workers, neighbors or even members of our family. In these cases, it is important to know how to set and enforce healthy, relational boundaries around ourselves to limit the degree of hurtful behavior directed at us. We need to gain confidence that it is OK to say, "NO, I won't tolerate being spoken to or treated in that manner. Period. If you continue to behave that way, I will have to remove myself from this relationship." The trick is having the strength and determination to follow through on the consequences we have promised. It helps when we learn how to set non-punitive, natural consequences. Doing so gives us reassurance that we are not just being mean and helps us to stand firm in the limits we have set. I do not want to portray that this is easy, it can be very hard. We will likely need the support and encouragement of others to follow through holding healthy boundaries. This is simply a thumbnail description of the principle.

So the first skill that will help us plan for a better future is learning how to recognize and avoid dangerous situations or people. The second area we need to approach in order to help people bring full resolution to the past and to have hope for a better future, is a little more personal. This involves helping a person discover possible sinful reactions on their part to being wronged. We are so used to thinking in black and white, *"If they did me wrong, they must be the bad guy. That makes me the good guy and everything I have done must be good and right."*

Well...this is not always the case. Sometimes we can make a legitimately bad situation worse by our own sinful reactions. Since we have a villain handy anyway, it is easy enough to shove all the blame for the whole mess on the other guy. In order for us to have greater confidence that we will not end up in a painful pit like this again, we have to address any part we played in digging the pit.

If we are hurt by someone, it seems natural to lash out at them, to judge them as being mean and evil, to warn everyone we can think of about how bad a person they are and to make them hurt like us. Besides, won't that help them learn to have empathy?

However, Scripture says that we are not to repay anyone evil for evil (Romans 12:17). We are not to judge people (Matthew 7:1, Luke 6: 37). True, we are to judge or discern the fruit a person grows, whether their actions are life giving or damaging. We are not to judge the person, their heart condition, their intentions and motives, the degree that they are good or evil. These are all abilities that are above our pay grade. Only God can know what's in a person's heart. Only He can know the extent to which they acted out of their own wounding or willful rebellion. When we do these things, we confuse our abilities with God's. We put ourselves in God's place. That is always a dangerous spot for a mere mortal. We are not to gossip (Romans 1:29, 2 Corinthians 12:20). God knows every detail of our own sinfulness. Thankfully, in His mercy, He does not go around telling everyone about it!

These reactions may be natural, but they are also damaging. They are damaging to those around us, and to us. Acting in these ways erodes our own character and spiritual health, poisoning our spirits; such reactions cause wounds in the lives of those around us. While we may feel completely justified and have it all rationalized in our minds, we are still responsible for continuing a chain reaction of injury being passed along throughout the human condition. So while the hurtful reactions are all natural, God invites us to participate in the supernatural. By the strength of His Holy Spirit we are called to restrain ourselves from sinful reactions to the sinful attacks against us. In the long run we are better off by not collaborating with the evil one to inflict further harm on ourselves after the initial injury.

So this is the process, more or less, that one will go through to experience healing of injuries done against the heart and soul: 1) Taking inventory: bringing into our own awareness what has been done against us; 2) Bringing it into the light: sharing with safe people our painful history and experiencing loving reactions; 3) Expressing emotions in non-destructive ways so the emotion can be processed and dissipated; 4) Releasing and forgiving: a process of letting go of our perceived rights to get justice or revenge and entrusting justice to God; 5) Inviting Jesus to heal the emotions locked away in our memories and to do for us what we cannot do for ourselves; and lastly 6) Planning for the future: both learning how to avoid avoidable hurts from predictably hurtful people and develop strategies for managing our own responses to being hurt so that we don't compound our situation with dysfunctional or sinful responses.

In the interest of full disclosure, I feel compelled to clarify something. By describing the process of healing in simple and clear terms, I do not mean to imply the process is always simple or easy. It can be difficult accounting for what you can't remember. Your subconscious has practiced selective memory for a long time and with good reason. Turning that around is not as simple as flipping a switch. Counselors have developed tools that can help recover lost information but the work of recalling may take time and effort. Expressing emotions and getting release may involve more than just a mental decision. Sometimes medicine is necessary to allow the brain to reboot after being stuck generating the neurotransmitters responsible for creating those unpleasant emotions. To get the mind to let go of very large traumas, techniques such as EMDR (eye movement desensitization and reprocessing) can serve as a manual rebooting option for the brain. A person can experience ambivalence about the healing process; wanting to be on the other side but unsure about going through the pain of recovery. Continued support may be needed to help rally the resolve and persistence necessary to stay with the process as long as is necessary. Forgiveness may need to be a decision made over and over with the encouragement and accountability of close confidants.

The process of healing is usually rigorous. But what I want to say here is that it is something that can be studied, understood and cooperated with. It can work. It usually happens as a process, over time. And experiencing the hope that making progress gives is much preferred to being stuck in a painful injury that cripples our ability to function, to experience God and to know the joy of life He intends us to have.

5

For Immaturity, There is Nurturing

It is not God's wish that we stay immature. The design we see in all nature is for things to grow up. What if we are immature, either because there were not people who knew how to nurture us or because we suffered from a Peter Pan complex (attempting to avoid growing up)? Either way, God wants to help us catch up. In Ephesians 4:11-16 Paul writes,

> *It was he (Jesus) who gave some to be apostles,*
> *some to be prophets, some to be evangelists, and*
> *some to be pastors and teachers, to prepare God's*
> *people for works of service, so that the body of Christ*
> *may be built up until we all reach unity in the faith*
> *and in the knowledge of the Son of God and become*
> *mature, attaining to the whole measure of the*
> *fullness of Christ.*
>
> *Then we will no longer be infants, tossed back*
> *and forth by the waves, and blown here and there*
> *by every wind of teaching and by the cunning*
> *and craftiness of men in their deceitful scheming.*

*Instead, speaking the truth in love, we will in all
things grow up into him who is the Head, that is,
Christ. From him the whole body, joined and held
together by every supporting ligament, grows and
builds itself up in love, as each part does its work.*

Paul describes the church acting as a new family who
gathers around us and helps us grow up. As a family, we
are connected. We help each other grow up. We do life
together growing strong in faith and wisdom. We become
capable of doing adult things.

People suffering from immaturity may need mentors, counselors, support/recovery groups, people who
will teach, model, affirm and correct. The truth is, we all
benefit from having mentors in our lives. Mentors give
developmentally appropriate homework assignments and
feedback on how we're progressing.

You would not ask a four-year-old child to complete a
long list of chores, like taking out the trash, cleaning the
bathroom, dusting and running the vacuum sweeper. You
might, however, ask them to put away their toys. On the
other hand, you would perhaps assign that same list of
chores to a ten-year-old child, though you would not ask
them to mow the lawn. You would save the more complicated jobs for when they are old enough to responsibly
handle a potentially dangerous machine. You reserve the
grass mowing, a bigger responsibility, for your teenage
child. You might also expect the teenager to get a part
time job and put money away in savings, though you

would not expect them to get a forty hour a week job and share equally the household expenses.

It works similarly for spiritual maturing. A person begins by having faith in the love of God expressed through Jesus and trusts His sacrifice as the source of rescue and restoration. The language familiar in the church is that a person is 'born again,' quoting what Jesus told Nicodemus. For a person who has just made a decision to accept Jesus as Lord of his life, we hold expectations appropriate for one who has just been born.

A newborn baby cannot do much that is overly productive. Mostly, they are good at crying and messing themselves. Veteran Christians often express frustration about the whining and complaining of some new Christians or chide them for their expectation that the church's primary role is to serve and satisfy *them*. "It's all about me" mentality is expected from a newborn. The problem is not so much the behavior of the new Christian, as the unrealistic expectations of the older siblings. We don't scold a baby for having a dirty diaper. We just eagerly await the time they can be potty trained. Until then, we care for them.

In a nurturing environment, there are realistic expectations about what is age appropriate ability. There is patience for the process of growing up. There is eagerness to teach, encourage and challenge as the developing Christian is able to receive and respond. The trait of a truly nurturing person or environment is the ability to challenge people toward more and more mature thoughts and behaviors while maintaining unconditional respect for the inherent worth in every person. We all need this kind of nurturing, because we are all subject to having areas that are underdeveloped. We were born into an imperfect world and an imperfect family.

Surrounded by a nurturing environment, a person grows in character through a process of mastering various acts of obedience to God as delineated in the Bible. In time, he grows more mature by practicing acts of sacrificial love.

An immature person matures over time with the guidance of a more mature person through tasks of gradually increasing challenge. This leads to maturity. Maturity leads to the ability to interact with God adult to adult, with greater closeness. Maturity allows us to be successful doing the adult things life requires of us. Maturity allows us to overcome the challenges of life and reduce the number of times *we* are the challenge for someone else.

It's not too hard to recognize when the people around us are acting immaturely. If you are feeling really brave though, you might do a little self-assessment of your own maturity. Ask yourself some of these questions. What are the areas of your spiritual life where you need to grow up a little? How are you doing with entitlement, expecting that God owes you more? How's your impulse control when it comes to waiting on God's answer to your prayers? Is it easy to wait on Him or are you tempted to run ahead and make your own way? How do you do with enduring legitimate suffering and pain? Can you trust God to be good and to bring good or do you avoid and medicate pain? How are you doing with carrying out adult responsibilities, obeying God's directives, giving generously your time, talent and money to further the Kingdom?

As you identify a character trait that needs development the next thing you need to do is to identify someone you see as more mature than you in that growth area. You want someone who is strong enough to challenge you forward without shaming you for being where you are. Sometimes it's a friend you already know. It might be a small group that's working together on the issue you need to work on. Sometimes we might benefit from someone with highly developed skills like a counselor or a spiritual director. It is worth finding nurturing people. It is truly exhilarating to grow and to reach new levels of mature abilities.

6

For Habits, There are Disciplines

Anyone who has tried to break a bad habit knows the least effective and most frustrating way to succeed is by trying to *not* do that thing. When the cravings hit, you think "don't do it, don't do it. I can't do it. I promised myself I wouldn't do it. I feel like I'm going to give in and do it, no, no, no... oops I did it!" By thinking about not doing "it", we end up obsessing about "it", which just tends to reinforce and strengthen the very thing we are trying not to do again!

If addiction is the mother of all bad habits, maybe we can learn something from those who have gained sobriety from their addiction. More than likely you've heard of the 12 steps:

Step 1 — Admitted we were powerless over our addiction—that our lives had become unmanageable

Step 2 — Came to believe that a Power greater than ourselves could restore us to sanity

Step 3 — Made a decision to turn our will and our lives over to the care of God as we understood God

Step 4 — Made a searching and fearless moral inventory of ourselves

Step 5 — Admitted to God, to ourselves and to another human being the exact nature of our wrongs

Step 6 — Were entirely ready to have God remove all these defects of character

Step 7 — Humbly asked God to remove our shortcomings

Step 8 — Made a list of all persons we had harmed, and became willing to make amends to them all

Step 9 — Made direct amends to such people wherever possible, except when to do so would injure them or others

Step 10 — Continued to take personal inventory and when we were wrong promptly admitted it

Step 11 — Sought through prayer and meditation to improve our conscious contact with God as we understood God, praying only for knowledge of God's will for us and the power to carry that out

Step 12 — Having had a spiritual awakening as the result of these steps, we tried to carry this message to other addicts, and to practice these principles in all our affairs

Addicts do not sit around thinking, "I'm not going to drink today, I'm not going to drink today." Instead, they meditate on these 12 steps. To avoid reinforcing the urge to drink, they strengthen their focus and commitment to doing these 12 things. They do not try to stop doing the habit. They replace old, bad habits with new, good habits. They do not try to *not* drink. Eventually, after months of working on the 12 steps, they find they aren't drinking. It's not easy, but the 12 steps make it possible for many people to be free.

In a broader context, we call these new, good habits "disciplines" or "spiritual disciplines." Richard Foster wrote the book Celebration of Discipline (Harper Collins Publishing) wherein he outlines and explains some of the core disciplines that Christians have practiced over centuries. These disciplines include: meditation, prayer, fasting, solitude, study, silence, confession, simplicity, worship, and service.

Most of us cringe when we think of disciplines, because they are challenging to do with regularity. We are prone to some, or all, of these extremes; being undisciplined, being lazy, or too busy. Each of these tendencies interferes with disciplines. Those who practice disciplines, find breakthroughs into greater strength. We see it in the sports world. Those athletes who discipline themselves to get up early to train, limit what they eat to nutritious foods and practice, practice, practice, are rewarded with abilities beyond their less dedicated competitors.

In the same way, people who practice spiritual disciplines are rewarded with an increased ability to perceive and experience God and the Kingdom of God on earth. Be careful that this does not slip into a 'works theology,' where you *earn* some greater blessing. This is not about becoming more deserving. This is about becoming more capable to participate in spiritual happenings.

Paul, when writing to his protégé Timothy, told him this...

For physical training is of some value, but godliness has value for all things, holding promise for both the present life and the life to come. This is a trustworthy saying that deserves full acceptance (and for this we labor and strive), that we have put our hope in the living God, who is the Savior of all men, and especially of those who believe. Command and teach these things. (1 Timothy 4:8-11)

Paul describes a training that is rigorous. We labor and strive. Our effort does not replace our hope in the saving power of Jesus. Training does enhance our experience with Jesus in a way that will have value and promise now and in the future life! Jesus' work makes relationship with Him possible. Our disciplines make the experience of that relationship more vital and rich. We see results in greater ability to live a life that enhances the lives of those around us, rather than burden them with the weight of the consequences of our bad habits.

What has been your experience with spiritual disciplines such as: meditation, prayer, fasting, solitude, study, silence, confession, simplicity, worship, service? Where have you struggled and where have you succeeded? What was the result of the times where you had some measure of success with spiritual disciplines?

What spiritual discipline do you feel led to pursue, either in study and/or practice?

7

For Oppression, There is Deliverance

The New Testament writer, James, wrote, *"Submit yourselves, then, to God. Resist the devil, and he will flee from you" (4:7)*. What specifically can we do to resist the devil and cause him to flee from us? What behaviors or decisions might work to deliver us from his oppressive influence? Here are four practical actions we can take to resist Satan:

- Recognize
- Repent
- Renounce
- Remain

Recognize — We may have to recognize events that have happened to us, choices we have made. We may need to consider behaviors in which we have engaged that gave the enemy permission and access to harass us. We do not always recognize when our choices are actually an agreement with the enemy. Coming into an agreement with the enemy, is sort of like entering into a contract with him. We give him certain rights and access to us. God's help might be required to recognize when this has happened. God may have to reveal things that we have repressed and forgotten. He will know how much we can bear to know, and in what order we need to work on things. First, we must decide to be willing to let Him show us.

Search me, O God, and know my heart; test me and know my anxious thoughts. See if there is any offensive way in me, and lead me in the way everlasting. (Psalm 139:23&24)

Here are some examples of things that can open doors for the enemy to attach himself to us and oppress us:

- Trauma against us, violence, rape, incest
- Consensual sex outside of marriage
- Trauma we committed against others, violence, homicide, abortion
- Bitterness, hatred, unforgiveness
- Fear
- Word curses spoken against us
- Occult involvement, Ouija board, horoscopes, séances/consulting the dead, casting spells, familiar spirits, spirit guides, witchcraft white or otherwise
- Generational history, curses and patterns

If any of these things have been part of our experience, we have to muster up the courage to own them as being part of our own personal history.

Repent — When I was a kid going to church, I used to hear Christians talk about the need to repent. They would get all serious-looking and angry-sounding. I don't know if they meant it this way, but in my mind at least, it sounded like, *"You awful sinner, repent! Repent I say, or you will certainly go to Hell!"* It didn't sound very kind to me, but actually more like a threat! I couldn't be altogether sure they weren't just a little bit happy with the thought of people going to Hell. It sounded like they were saying, *"You rejected what we were pushing on you and wouldn't repent like we told you, so I'm glad you're going to Hell. Good! It serves you right!"* They certainly scared me! I tried to be the very best little boy I could.

I wasn't the only one who didn't take kindly to the threats. I saw a lot of folks react to such intimidation by saying, *"I'll show you! You can't push me around and tell me what to do! Who do you think you are? I'm going to do what I want to do."* I can understand their reaction against being bossed around by self-righteous people. But it doesn't seem to work out well when people assert their autonomy from religious bullies by revolting against God's counsel. When people ignore what God is saying, they invite extra trouble into their lives. I lived in fear of God, but I never experienced the catastrophic conse-quences of my friends who ignored God. I never went to jail. I never got thrown out of my house. I finished school, got a job, paid my bills, avoided divorce. All that seemed better than the alternative of doing the opposite of what God has said just to show someone I won't be bossed around. I do however understand people resisting the threat to repent, as I didn't like being bullied either.

Recently, I started seeing this thing called *repentance* differently. I knew by definition, it meant to turn away from living a godless, selfish, disobedient life. When I started to read what Jesus actually said about repentance, it had a very different tone than what I remembered hearing from other people.

In the Gospel of Matthew Chapter 4 it says:

[17]From that time on Jesus began to preach, "Repent, for the kingdom of heaven is near."

In the Gospel of Mark, it records the same thing this way:

[14]After John was put in prison, Jesus went into Galilee, proclaiming the good news of God. [15]"The time has come," he said. "The kingdom of God is near. Repent and believe the good news!"

One day, I was thinking about this idea of repenting and what Jesus might be saying. I remembered some news stories I would hear periodically about people visiting a nearby state park that has a beautiful river gorge. The river has cut a deep canyon in the rocks there and there are trails that take you from parking areas to the very edge of the canyon. The view when standing on the cliffs of the canyon ridge of the valley below is beautiful. Though there are designated camping sites for hikers, many have chosen instead to camp close to the top of the canyon, so they will have beautiful scenery right from their camp. After an evening of sitting around the campfire, drinking a few too many beers, they wake up in the middle of the night, and have to do what you gotta do when you drank a lot before going to bed. Half asleep, and a little groggy from the beer, they head down the trail in the dark and walk right off the cliff, falling to their death.

I got to thinking, "What if Jesus' kind of repentance is like this: He sees me in the dark, spiritually speaking, walking down a path, looking for some relief. He knows the path I am on will lead to my destruction. He calls out to me, *"Mark, stop where you are! There's danger that way. Turn around. Come back. Come here to the sound of my voice. The party is this way. Come join the party!"* This is a better fit with Jesus' words, *"Repent, for the kingdom of heaven is near."* The Kingdom is God's party.

To make sure this new way of thinking about repenting was right, I looked further in the Bible and found this story Jesus told in Luke Chapter 15:

> *3Then Jesus told them this parable: 4"Suppose one of you has a hundred sheep and loses one of them. Does he not leave the ninety-nine in the open country and go after the lost sheep until he finds it? 5And when he finds it, he joyfully puts it on his shoulders 6and goes home. Then he calls his friends and neighbors together and says, 'Rejoice with me; I have found my lost sheep.' 7I tell you that in the same way there*

will be more rejoicing in heaven over one sinner who repents than over ninety-nine righteous persons who do not need to repent.

By Jesus' account, the sheep is *lost*, not awful or bad. Jesus' reaction is not anger. He "joyfully puts us on His shoulders and carries us back to safety." Anger is not the prevailing feeling God has for us. Joy is. The angels rejoice and celebrate. As it turns out, the call to repent is not a threat. His call to repent is a warning and an invitation, given in love.

The danger, the cliff, is not just going to Hell. The destruction Jesus is trying to save us from is the destruction of our lives that happens here, in this life, by our own hands. He is talking about the way a life turns out when we live selfishly, doing things our way, apart from God's direction. I have seen it myself, *in* myself. When I live by what seems natural to me, it is usually selfish, and it usually does not work out well. When I think about what God has asked me to do, it is often harder to do. It does not come as naturally to me. If, however, I do as He asks, I like myself and my life better. I feel closer to God. I feel His love for me. I feel like I'm able to show love back to Him.

Repenting is not just turning *away* from bad behavior to good behavior. Repenting is a *turning around*. Even knowing this, it is hardly ever enough motivation for me. I am too attracted to behaving badly. Repenting is turning from alliance with Satan who wants to destroy me. Repenting is turning away from independence and separation from God in my own ignorance. Repenting is turning back to *inter*dependence with God who cares for me. Now, this *does* motivate me. Coming into agreement with God about what is good and what is evil, agreeing with God about the damage that's caused by evil, is worth getting on board!

Jesus is sending out an invitation, *"The kingdom of God is near, in all its goodness and glory. You are invited in, to participate and to perpetuate it in the Earth. You have to reorient yourself. If you are turned away from God, turn back to Him. Come near to Him."* This is repentance.

Renounce — People in the process of becoming naturalized citizens, must renounce allegiance to their birth nation. They are relinquishing the rights and privileges associated with being a citizen of the country of their birth, in exchange for the rights and privileges of being a citizen of their newly chosen country. We must relinquish the rights and privileges of agreement with Satan for the privileges of being in union with God. The writer of Hebrews gives Moses as an example.

By faith Moses, when he had grown up, refused to be known as the son of Pharaoh's daughter. He chose to be mistreated along with the people of God rather than to enjoy the pleasures of sin for a short time. He regarded disgrace for the sake of Christ as of greater value than the treasures of Egypt, because

> *he was looking ahead to his reward. By faith he left*
> *Egypt, not fearing the king's anger; he persevered*
> *because he saw him who is invisible. By faith he kept*
> *the Passover and the sprinkling of blood, so that*
> *the destroyer of the firstborn would not touch the*
> *firstborn of Israel. (Hebrews 11:24-28)*

I realized I was oppressed by worry. When it came time to renounce my agreement with the Devil, I had to figure out what rights and privileges I was relinquishing. I discovered worry gave me the impression that if I maintained constant vigilance about the future, I could avoid painful events. When I identified my assumed benefit from worry, I saw my error. Even with my vigilance, I do not have the power to stop much of anything. Knowing this made it easier to renounce my commitment to worry. I then had to identify what my new rights and privileges would be.

> *Humble yourselves, therefore, under God's mighty*
> *hand, that he may lift you up in due time. Cast*
> *all your anxiety on him because he cares for you.*
> *Be self-controlled and alert. Your enemy the devil*
> *prowls around like a roaring lion looking for*
> *someone to devour. Resist him , standing firm in*
> *the faith,... (1 Peter 5:6-9)*

If I would humble myself and admit that unlike God, I cannot know everything and cannot control everything,

I could then choose to trust God with my concerns, knowing that He cares for me. There is great comfort there. Paul confirmed it when he wrote in Philippians 4:6-7,

Do not be anxious about anything, but in everything, by prayer and petition, with thanksgiving, present your requests to God. And the peace of God, which transcends all understanding, will guard your hearts and your minds in Christ Jesus.

Remain — When we get free, it is wise to continue the kind of behaviors that brought freedom, and avoid the behaviors that invite oppression.

A prayer might go something like this:

"Father I recognize that my fear and worry reveal a lack of trust in you. They are an insult to your goodness and your faithfulness. I'm sorry, and I ask your forgiveness. I forgive my family, who modeled and helped instill fear in me. I release them. With the help of your Holy Spirit, I commit myself to faith and trust in you for all uncertainties in my future. You, alone, know what lies ahead and are powerful enough to do something about it. I turn toward you and your care for me. I renounce the agreement made with the enemy when I chose to participate in worry and fear. I renounce all rights and privileges promised to me openly or implied. I worship you, God, for your forgiveness,

*your patience and goodness to me and for planning
a future for me. I ask your help, Holy Spirit, in
establishing a new habit of trust in place of worry.
Amen."*

Perhaps in one of your next quiet times of meditation
you might ask God to reveal any open doors there may
be in your past or present that are giving access to the
enemy to oppress you. Make a list of possible entry points
that come to mind. With each item on the list, record how
that past experience takes you away from God and how
it would look for you to turn back towards God regarding
this issue. Identify any rights, privileges or advantages
you got from your agreement to participate with the enemy. Also, identify any promises God has made for taking
care of you regarding this issue.

Consider praying a prayer such as this:

*Father, I recognize these things as being possible
entry points for the enemy to harass and oppress
me...(from your list)*

*I agree with you that this is other than what
you have for me and I'm sorry. Please forgive me. I
renounce my agreement and participation in...*

*I commit myself to you God and to your ways.
Holy Spirit please help me to live with you by your
guidance and your strength. Keep me alert to the
enemy's attempts to re-engage me in this trap. Help
me to remain in the truth. I celebrate your kindness*

to me, Father. Thanks for your love and forgiveness.
In the name of Christ we pray amen.

As you've been reading about God's solutions to what can go wrong in us people have more than likely come to mind who live out of obvious brokenness and immaturity. You might know someone that is possibly experiencing spiritual oppression of some kind. We all know people who are stuck in bad habits. It's always easier to see the problems other people have. It's tempting to focus on other people's issues rather than addressing our own. But if you actually consider doing this kind of work, it becomes apparent that doing it alone may be nearly impossible. When we seriously think about opening ourselves up to God's solutions for what's wrong with us, it's easy to see why small groups can be such an effective way of growing toward wholeness.

In small groups, we can study and learn all the secrets God has revealed in His scriptures about how to live life. In a small group, we can process and wrestle with what it will mean to apply God's truths. We can get encouragement and accountability when struggling. We have someone with whom we can celebrate breakthroughs. In a healthy, functional small group we see others model how to live in an area that we have yet to master. We have people to challenge us to keep going when we get discouraged or weary. We have people to go with us on the journey. There are people to pray with and for us, to invite and invoke God's power to do what we cannot do for ourselves.

Small groups can be a vehicle that provides elements of all four solutions to address all four parts of "What is *wrong* with people?!" Any church that specializes in only one or two elements, will only be able to help *some* of the people, *some* of the time. A church that is a great teaching church will help *some* of the people, *some* of the time. A church that specializes in deliverance ministry will help *some* of the people, *some* of the time. A church with a counseling ministry will help *some* of the people, *some* of the time. These churches will help a segment of humanity being overlooked by other churches. However, unless the church addresses all four elements together, healing, nurturing, disciplines and deliverance, she will still be limited to partial success.

Having a full understanding and ability to practice skills in all four areas of God's remedies is the secret to helping *more* people, *more* of the time. Notice, I say *"more people"* and not *"all people."* There is still the element of free will. Even after being offered help in all four areas, some will still choose a life style that is both harmful to others and self-destructive. For those who desire to change their lives, the church can be more effective in escorting them into wholeness and maturity.

8

Toto, We're Not in Kansas Anymore!

The first and best use of the remedies for "What is *wrong* with people?!" is self-directed. We have the most to gain by examining our own condition, identifying our own areas of wounding, immaturity, habits and negative spiritual influence. As we discover and address these issues in ourselves, we become stronger and more whole. From a place of strength and wholeness, we possess the greatest potential to impact our culture positively. We should probably start and spend most of our energy, there. After doing all the work we can do on ourselves, we still have to interact with other people. We will still have to endure and survive the brokenness, immaturity, bad habits and spiritual darkness of those we live alongside. What is the application of these ideas when dealing with the people around us?

I will address one of the more challenging situations we are likely to face. The principles that work in this difficult scenario will also serve us in easier circumstances.

My friend Marie was working with a sweet lady in our church named Paulette. [1]Paulette served faithfully for many years. She was well known and well liked, and was given positions of greater and greater responsibility and influence, because of the success of her ministry over the years.

There came a time when things started getting squirrely in dealing with Paulette. It was very subtle at first. Little things began to emerge; things not so unlike what every other leader in our ministry was experiencing. There were some personal issues. The environment in Paulette's home was becoming stressful. Relationships were growing strained.

Marie began to get feedback about the ministry where Paulette was serving. There were reports of conflict and dissatisfaction among the team. These kinds of personal and ministry issues are pretty natural, so Marie did not really feel concerned at first. After all, Paulette had been a trusted Christian leader for quite a while. She was part of a small group, so if there was a problem, surely someone would notice, right?

Well, that is exactly how it came to light—in the context of a small group, but only after some time. It was the small group of fellow leaders who recognized a pattern that persisted, despite the feedback and encouragement of the group. As we have strong guidelines against

---

1 Paulette was not a particular person, but was a composite of various people we had encountered.

gossip, people were reluctant to say much when they had unpleasant encounters with Paulette. Besides, none of the instances were so big a deal that they couldn't be forgiven. In an effort to show grace, her team mates chose to simply give her the benefit of the doubt and move past the offense, which is exactly what we would hope for in most circumstances.

As Paulette's supervisor, it was Marie's job to inspect Paulette's ministry performance. Marie noticed a trend emerging that could not be ignored. Certain behaviors were having a negative impact on Paulette's teammates and the folks they were trying to serve. It was clear that the pattern of behaviors were not serving Paulette all that well either. In fact, it was becoming more obvious these behaviors were the tip of an iceberg; an issue that was causing Paulette a significant degree of suffering as well. Marie decided she would need to speak with Paulette about what was happening.

I should clarify. I would not identify anything as being especially problematic beyond the norm. It is what happened next that I want to lift up for our consideration and learning. Marie prepared herself for talking with Paulette. She made a list of behaviorally specific examples of the incidences that gave rise for concern. She was careful to avoid labels about Paulette's personhood or character and stuck with descriptions of behavior and the consequences. Marie processed her own frustrations in connection with some of the events, so she could approach Paulette as emotionally neutral as possible. Marie prepared a list of genuine affirmations as well, to give Paulette credit for all the good she was doing. Marie hoped to affirm her respect and appreciation for Paulette, while also offering insight into what was likely a blind spot for her regarding the impact of some of her actions on those around her.

Marie did all the things we do when we are giving someone a constructive critique intended to lead them on to greater and greater success in the work they are doing. Marie practiced all the tools that typically work very well. She entered into the meeting with Paulette with hopeful optimism. She left the meeting with perplexing confusion. Marie did not get the result she was expecting. She did not get the reaction we were used to getting.

Marie did not get a commitment to grow and improve. Marie did not get thanks for a gentle invitation to see into a blind spot. Instead, Marie received a blast of anger and accusation. Paulette ran through a long list of many wrongs Marie had done against her, though this was the first mention or even hint of displeasure. Paulette finished her barrage of rage by getting up and storming out of the meeting.

Marie reviewed her preparation. She checked to see if her language had been objective and non-inflammatory. She checked her heart to see if she had any unaccounted for emotions that were slipping out in the dialogue. She ran what happened in the meeting past a trusted colleague who also cared for Paulette and wanted to see her succeed. Marie ran her plan for the next meeting past her accountability partner. She was confident she had not made any obvious blunders, and sure that the plan for the follow up meeting was true and clean. Surely, the first meeting was a fluke. She must have caught Paulette on a bad day. This time would be much better! And yet, it wasn't.

It got worse. When Marie asked Paulette to be a part of the work of the ministry, she was accused of only wanting Paulette for what she could do and didn't care about how exhausted Paulette was. When Marie suggested she take a break, Paulette accused Marie of not valuing her contribution and firing her. Paulette accused Marie of neglecting her, even though it was Paulette who missed several of the team meetings Marie had scheduled. Marie set up individual appointments for Paulette that she either no-showed or cancelled at the last minute. Marie was feeling like she was in a no-win situation, and she was.

Filled with self-doubt and confounded about how things were going, Marie and I began to review in detail all that had happened. In the course of examining the previous events, I had an intuitive impression about what might be happening. Dorothy, from the Wizard of Oz, came to mind, specifically the quote, *"Toto, we're not in Kansas anymore!"* You see, it was a very helpful observation that Dorothy made. The recognition that she was not in her familiar homeland, but was in a new and foreign place, allowed her to do two things. First, she could begin to suspend her expectations that things should or would be exactly as they were at home. Secondly, she could open up her power of observations to capture and account for the unexpected. To continue to expect what would normally happen in Kansas would not help her. To be ready for something completely new would serve her well.

I began to suspect that we had journeyed out of our homeland to where the rules and parameters to which we were accustomed no longer applied or worked. Clearly, they were not working. We had to figure out what the new rules were, and how they differed from what we were expecting. This is what we came away with.

It is easiest to start with the familiar, with what we expect to be the norm. In *our* homeland, people say what they mean and mean what they say; they do what they say they are going to do; they ask for what they want; they say "yes" to what they are willing to agree to, and "no" to what they are not in agreement with. In our homeland, people recognize a good person can do dumb things; that doing something wrong does not make a person bad; that if you are the one who has done something bad, you own up to it, ask for forgiveness and make amends; that if someone has wronged you, you point it out respectfully and forgive readily. In our homeland, if what you are doing is not working, you do something different; if what you are doing is working, you do more of it. This is how things are done in our homeland; where we live and work; where we are from. We thought it reasonable and rational to expect others would have the same language and values in relationship with us.

Now, this is what the rules seemed to be in this foreign land. If someone cares about you, they should be able to read your mind and anticipate what you want. My own preferences are the requirements by which all others are to be judged. If someone else has different preferences, they are being selfish. Under no circumstances do you admit guilt of anything. If someone presents you with evidence that you are guilty of doing wrong, blame circumstances or another person. If they press the matter in presenting evidence of your guilt, shift the blame to them. Make assertions about their heart and their motives, as though they were indisputable fact. Wait until enough time has passed for memories to become faded, and rewrite history in your favor. If in any discussion you begin losing a disagreement, fall back to an explosive, emotional outburst. Anger works best. If anger does not drive the attacker away, play the part of a victim to get sympathy, so they will leave you alone. If that does not work, cut off from relationship and accuse them of rejecting you. You shall be committed to these rules without regard to whether they are working or not. These appeared to be the rules of engagement in a foreign land, but they seemed crazy to us!

With these insights came clarity. The rules were crazy, because we had entered Crazyville. In Crazyville, these rules make perfect sense. They are completely consistent within themselves. They only look crazy when viewed from our homeland, Normal (not the one in Illinois). This is the tricky part; most citizens of Crazyville are used to visiting Normal. When they come for a visit, they know the traditions and enough of the language they are able to act accordingly for short periods of time. Be aware, while you are interacting with them, they may lure you across the city limits. Unbeknownst to you, you have crossed over into their land where their rules apply. In that moment, they have the home court advantage. While they may have some experience and proficiency with the rules in Normal, you may have little experience or mastery with the rules of Crazyville. You are out gunned and out matched.

Now, I must fess up at this point. In theory, it seems very clear. In practice, it is more complicated. The truth is we all have the potential for living in Crazyville. Some of us live there full time. Some of us are part-time residents. Some of us take extended vacations there. Some of us only visit there on special occasions, possibly returning for holidays with our families of origin who have never moved from there! Any one of us, given the right situation, the right circumstances, because of our unique history, is capable of acting out of our own brand of weird, crazy dysfunction. To what degree we live there, depends on the amount of injury, immaturity, bad habits and spiritual oppression we have experienced and how much healing, nurturing, discipline and deliverance we have embraced.

This can serve as a little test to help you discern who has been visiting Crazyville. If you are in a conflictual relationship that is driving you crazy, ask yourself this, *"How many other relationships do I have that are causing me this same level of distress?"* If you can identify a few relationships that have some similar patterns, you could be the common denominator. It could be *your* craziness that is causing the disharmony. You may want to ask some close trusted friends for some honest feedback, and then brace yourself for what you are about to hear.

Is this is the only relationship that is going so badly? Do you have other relationships where you are known deeply and have been known for a significant time; relationships where no one has called out a problem in your attitudes or behaviors? If so, that is a strong indicator that the craziness of your conflictual relationship is coming from the other person. It is reassuring to be able to do this kind of perspective check, because citizens of Crazyville can be very convincing in their assertions that you are the main problem. It is worse, if there are several of them working together, as in some families or some toxic faith communities. You may, in fact, be the odd man or woman out, which can make it seem like *you* must be the problem. When, in fact, you are just in the town square of Crazyville.

9

Escape from Crazyville

Suppose there is a person you find yourself in regular conflict with. What if it is someone especially important to you, a friend, a family member or someone in your church community? You cannot help but wonder, *"How do I help them escape Crazyville?"* If you have any compassion for them, you want to see them set free. You may have already tried several times to help them, but you keep hitting a wall.

We can find a clue about what to do from the world of air travel. If you have ever been on an airplane, you have no doubt heard the safety speech the flight attendants dutifully deliver at the beginning of each flight. If you travel often, you may be so accustomed to it you block it out while settling into your seat, searching for some interesting reading.

The flight attendants explain, *"In the event of a loss in cabin pressure, oxygen masks will drop from the panels in the ceiling. If they appear, place the cup over your own nose and mouth , to better enable you to assist others."* At first hearing, this may seem very selfish and uncaring, especially if you are travelling with small children. The reality is that you have but a few seconds without oxygen before you will pass out. If you pass out, you are of no help to anyone else nearby, especially the very young, the elderly or those unable to help themselves. You *must* first ensure you are able to help others. *Not* safeguarding yourself first is irresponsible, and by *not* doing so, you put others at risk.

So it is with any attempt to help someone escape from Crazyville. You must first make your own escape from the dizzying and confusing effects of the craziness. Only from a place of rational clarity can you be of any help to someone gripped in the dysfunction of Crazyville. I have missed this myself on occasion. Unaware of what was going on, I found myself hooked by the heat of emotion, prevalent in such interactions. Soon, I was triggered by the false accusations that I was not doing enough, or that I was the main source of the problem.

Even though I maintained enough self-control to refrain from a tit-for-tat exchange, I was still emotionally activated to a degree. I lost the ability to think clearly and extend the peace the other person needed to calm down and, possibly, engage in a rational conversation.

What can I do to control my own emotional reaction and ensure my response is most helpful? First, I begin with a little self-talk to keep myself grounded. I might tell myself things like, *"This feels like an attack, but it is not personal. This is probably the coping skill this person uses with most people, when they feel threatened. Their actions and words are more reflective of them than they are of me. Their reactions indicate that this person may be hurt and scared. They need someone strong enough to endure their hurtful patterns of relating if they have any chance of breaking free. Perhaps, I can be strong enough to be a person who helps them.*" By telling myself these things, I can reduce the chance of reacting emotionally myself, and increase my chance to respond thoughtfully.

Part of my thoughtful response will be to decline to play the game by their rules. I may not be able to convince them to play by the rules that guide me. However, I *can* decide to differentiate myself from assertions about me that are not true, historical accounts about what has happened between us that are not accurate, and declarations about future events that are not so certain. I do not have to argue the person into submission. I just declare that I have a different perspective and a different code by which I do relationships. I can limit my assertions to behaviorally specific observations, such as, "I hear you saying this issue between us is because of what I have done. I do not hear you taking any ownership for what you may have contributed to our conflict." I can avoid making blanket statements about them like, "You are just impossible," or "You never think you have done anything wrong."

The kind of response they give you, will reveal what type of person you are working with. Someone who is able to hear a differing point of view, acknowledge any valid points you have made and who will admit points of agreement might be willing to negotiate a mutually agreeable solution in light of the remaining differences. Such a person is probably from Normal. With this person, you can have conversation and work toward resolution of conflict. If the person erupts at any attempt to have an open, honest discussion and remains entrenched in their highly subjective and distorted interpretations, you are most likely dealing with someone from Crazyville. Civil discourse is not likely with a Crazyville resident, and attempts will probably not be productive.

If normal discussion will not work, what can a person do once they suspect they have been lured into Crazyville? Your best course of action is to invite the person to entertain the notion of healing, maturity, discipline and spiritual freedom. Attempt to make the invitation as compelling as possible. Do this by avoiding actions and words that will certainly trigger a negative reaction. Be sure to set and enforce healthy boundaries.

Dr. Henry Cloud wrote about this in his book, _Necessary Endings_. He describes a wise person, a foolish person and an evil person. A wise person, when presented with the light that reveals a need for change, will change his attitudes and behaviors. We would say that person is from Normal. You can interact with him in normal ways and expect positive results. A foolish person, when presented with the light revealing the need for change, will attempt to change the light. He will rationalize, excuse, deny and go to extensive effort to avoid changing. We would say he is from Crazyville. Normal discussions will not work. Boundaries may present enough discomfort that he might change his behavior. His attitudes may not change, because he may care little about you, or possibly anyone else, but his behavior might.

An evil person *cares nothing about the light,* and is only thinking about his own wants. He is either indifferent or may even enjoy the pain his actions bring to those around him. This person may be so unsafe they have been forced to the outskirts of Crazyville. Dr. Cloud advises quarantine, which may be accomplished by removing yourself from contact with the individual, as is possible.

I should probably warn you about something regarding what happens after a boundary is set. Some people find it hard to set boundaries. It is just not in their nature to say "no" to someone, to *anyone*! They prefer to be what they consider is agreeable, and say "yes" as much as possible. The fact is, there are times when "no" *is* the right answer. As hard as you may find it to set boundaries with someone, your work is not done at the point you have declared your boundary.

What if someone has a history of successfully manipulating or bullying you emotionally? What if this time you say, "No. I will not tolerate that kind of treatment anymore!"? Does it really seem likely they will think, "I guess I won't get away with that anymore"? More likely, their thought will be, "I wonder how serious they are about this? I bet I can still get my way if I increase the pressure." You should be prepared to have your boundary tested soon after you have declared it.

It is also important to remember boundaries are not intended to control *another person's* behavior. Boundaries help us control *our* behavior in the face of treatment that is unkind or hurtful. "You are not allowed to hurt me anymore," is not an effective boundary. You *can* say, "If you scream at me, I will have to leave until we can resume a calm conversation. I do not have conversations with people who yell at me." The next time they begin yelling, you will need to remind them of your boundary, stand up and walk away. The objective of boundary setting is not to inflict punishment to motivate someone to change. Boundaries protect you by limiting the amount of destructive behavior allowed to enter into your world. Sometimes, the adjustment you make by changing the way you participate in the relationship does create enough discomfort that the other person can find motivation to change their behavior.

When you declare what behavior you will not accept, it is helpful to say what you want. Using the statement in the example above, "I will not accept yelling, I want calm conversation," we see this is inviting the person to engage with me in a new way. By setting and enforcing boundaries which may create discomfort, I am making the invitation to practice new behavior more compelling. Regardless, it is still an invitation. I cannot insist someone change. I can only insist they modify their behavior, if they wish to continue being in relationship with me.

What makes the invitation compelling is the fact that I am modeling the kind of behavior that *is* normal. Some people do what they do because it is all they know to do.

They may have never seen a better way done. They may have never been taught a healthier means. By demonstrating what makes a normal, healthy relationship, you give the person a vision of another possible option. Having seen something else, they may choose to do *other* than what they have always done before.

Here is one last secret. After doing everything you know to do to encourage a better relationship, the person may still choose to maintain residence in Crazyville. When I am coaching people in situations like this, they frequently ask the question, "What else do I do now?" My answer is, "Nothing. Nothing else." There are times when you have done all you can do to encourage a positive change. Now, it is the other person's move. Will they decide to do differently this time? There may not be anything new to add to your repertoire of relational practices, except to continue doing the best you know to do. What might make the invitation compelling is that you are consistent and persistent. It may take a while for some people to be convinced you are serious about changing the nature of your relationship. After some time of testing, though, they may conclude that you say what you mean, and you mean what you say. If they want to continue to be in relationship with you, they are going to have to make corrections.

10
Last Thoughts

So perhaps what is wrong with those people around us who astound and aggravate us is more complicated than the notion that they are deciding to be irresponsible and irritating. And perhaps what's wrong with us is more complex than "I'm a loser who is messed up in a way greater than all the other people around me." It seems universal that we have vital needs for nurture and training that go unmet. This creates deficits of character and ability to live life successfully. As good as any one person may have had it, no one had perfect parents or a perfect upbringing. The best of parents may have lacked an essential life skill, and, therefore, could not pass on to their children completely healthy, life-giving tools. We are all missing something valuable that we need.

There is reason to believe that the deficiencies and injuries we experience in our youth are not by accident. It is not paranoia, if someone really is out to get you! What is wrong with people is that there is a malevolent, spiritual being, who intends us harm. If you have heard the stories of very many people, it is not hard to see a cold, calculated, malicious strategy, aimed at destroying humanity. This sounds melodramatic, until you begin to recognize the scope of the assault on the human soul, beginning at birth. Some, in fact, are convinced this assault actually begins in utero, well before birth. The attack on the identity begins while a person is young and vulnerable. Harsh words spoken in anger, judgments, unrealistic expectations and bullying are common memories for most of us. Experiencing childhood abuse of a mental, emotional, physical or even sexual nature, is even worse. With deep-heart wounds inflicted so early in life, before coping skills have been developed, the victim may go on to be a predator, and a vicious cycle is initiated.

Wedges are driven between the person and their loving Creator. Every effort is made by the evil one to widen the rift, as the years go by. If a person perceives they are lost from God's care, they tend to drift farther and farther away from the only source of love that is strong enough to repair and redeem the damage caused to the spirit.

If a great but partial remedy is offered, there will still be a failure to reach our potential. We cannot pray away immaturity. We cannot educate away spiritual harassment. We cannot work hard enough to heal our own wounds. We need a comprehensive solution if we want a thorough restoration to whom and what we were meant to be. It is much easier to do one part very well than it is to do all parts effectively. That is why there are churches known for being great teaching churches or great healing churches or passionate deliverance churches. I'm trying to think of a church with a great reputation for being well balanced among healing, nurturing, spiritual disciplines and deliverance. I'm having trouble naming one that's famous for this. There may be churches out there, but I think they're held suspect more than they are celebrated.

There are some people who spend their entire lives focused on eliminating their weaknesses. They conduct one fearless, moral inventory after another. They become completely willing to have God reveal their character defects. Even with complete intentionality and focus, they may continue to relapse into an addiction, fault or sin that will plague them. It is just not enough to focus on eliminating our weaknesses. Healing addresses weakness, and that is good. Nurturing and disciplines, however, build strength. After a surgery to repair an injured and weakened body part, physical therapy and rehab are prescribed to build strength. A person is not declared well, until both weakness is removed and strength is regained.

I understand why most introductions in a 12-step meeting begin with, *"Hi, I'm Mark and I'm an alcoholic."* The strategy is to remind an addict that he will, for the rest of his life, have a vulnerability he must always be on guard to defend against. But are we truly best defined by our greatest injury or our biggest scar? Is this the identity we were meant to have or could there be something more? What if we went past eliminating the weakness, and moved into developing the strength God desired to give? Could we not move into a greater destiny and a larger identity? How wonderful it would be to have a world full of people declaring, "*My name is..., and I'm an artist, a pioneer, a leader, a mentor, a healer, a craftsman, a problem solver, a father, a mother.*"

Healing of weakness must be met with the building of strength. The only way to do this successfully is to selectively and carefully choose those we will align ourselves with. We must prayerfully and thoughtfully choose whom we will ask to help us. In the same way we would exercise care in selecting the right doctor or the right coach, we must consider where our spiritual help is coming from. When we do not intentionally choose to find our help in God, it automatically comes from the other side. There is really no such thing as '*going it alone.*' Without God's protection, the evil one sweeps in to offer his "help."

While injury, immaturity, bad habits and spiritual oppression can all diminish one's capacity to use free will, our volition will always be an important factor. I must be willing to do an accurate accounting of the injuries I have experienced and to feel the pain long suppressed. I must be willing to forgive those through whom these injuries have come. I must be willing to seek out mentors who are more mature than I. I must be willing to receive instruction, take direction, accept assignments, hear critique and apply correction. I must be willing to practice restraint and self-denial. I must commit to doing that which is not easy or convenient and must learn to do these things with regularity and consistency. I must be willing to acknowledge there are realities that transcend the material world and cannot be measured in feet, pounds or gallons. I must decide with which side I will align myself—with darkness or with light. Disregarding all else, I must at least be willing to be made willing.

I learned a valuable prayer from my 12-step friends... The Serenity Prayer:

God grant me the serenity to accept the things I cannot change, the courage to change the things I can, and the wisdom to tell the difference.

I have a similar prayer that I use regularly in my attempt to be part of the solution and not part of the problem of what's wrong with people. My version goes like this:

God grant me the humility to allow You to do for me what I cannot do for myself, the courage to do what is my part, and the will to join You in this mystical partnership. Amen.

References

The following books were useful for provoking thought. Their listing here does not endorse every idea their authors have espoused but simply acknowledges their influence upon the writing of this book.

Bitarri, Pablo. Free In Christ. Charisma House, 2000

Boyd, Greg. Is God to Blame. Inter-varsity Pres, 2003

Cloud, Henry and Townsend, John. Safe People. Zondervan, 1996

Cloud, Dr. Henry. Necessary Endings. Zondervan, 2010

Cloud, Henry and Townsend, John.Boundaries. Zondervan, 1992

Foster, Richard. Celebration of Discipline. Harperone, 1998

Sandford, John & Paula. Healing the Wounded Spirit. Bridge Publishing, Inc, 1985

Wright, Henry. A More Excellent Way. Whitaker House Publishers, 2009

CPSIA information can be obtained
at www.ICGtesting.com
Printed in the USA
FFOW05n1433220115